GOSPEL
THE BOOK OF
LUKE

A NEW TRANSLATION WITH COMMENTARY—
JESUS SPIRITUALITY FOR EVERYONE

GOSPEL
THE BOOK OF
LUKE

THOMAS MOORE

Walking Together, Finding the Way®
SKY**LIGHT** PATHS®
PUBLISHING
Nashville, Tennessee

SkyLight Paths Publishing
an imprint of Turner Publishing Company
Nashville, Tennessee
New York, New York
www.skylightpaths.com
www.turnerpublishing.com

Gospel—The Book of Luke:
A New Translation with Commentary—Jesus Spirituality for Everyone

2018 Hardcover, First Printing
© 2018 by Thomas Moore

For information regarding permission to reprint material from this book, please write or fax your request to Turner Publishing, Permissions Department, at 4507 Charlotte Avenue, Suite 100, Nashville, Tennessee 37209, (615) 255-2665, fax (615) 255-5081, or email your request to submissions@turnerpublishing.com.

Library of Congress Cataloging-in-Publication Data

Names: Moore, Thomas, 1940- translator, commentator.
Title: The book of Luke : a new translation with commentary ; Jesus
  spirituality for everyone / Thomas Moore.
Other titles: Bible. Luke. English. Moore. 2017.
Description: Nashville, Tennessee : Turner Publishing, 2017. | Series: Gospel
  | Includes bibliographical references.
Identifiers: LCCN 2017042983 | ISBN 9781594736384 (hardcover)
Subjects: LCSH: Bible. Luke--Commentaries.
Classification: LCC BS2593 .M66 2017 | DDC 226.4/05209--dc23
LC record available at https://lccn.loc.gov/2017042983

10 9 8 7 6 5 4 3 2 1
Manufactured in the United States

Cover Design: Jenny Buono
Interior Design: Tim Holtz

To Abe

Contents

Introduction to Gospel

Why a New Translation?

In my travels I have met many people who grew up hearing the Gospels in church and have now moved on in a different direction. Some have found their religion outmoded or just do not feel like participating any longer. Some have been offended, like many women who find formal religion sexist. Others are attracted to altogether different traditions, and some do not see the point of religion at all.

Many told me they missed the stories and the teachings, and wished they could have a better, more up-to-date understanding of them. I have heard from other people who did not have a Christian background and wondered if the Gospels could add to their more open-ended spiritual path. I have strong empathy for both positions and wanted to present the Gospels in a way that would speak to both.

Some Christians, both traditional and independent, expressed their fervent curiosity about how I might understand the teachings, given my unusual background as a monk, a student of world religions, and a depth psychotherapist. I felt their eagerness and sincerity when they asked me to recommend a good translation. I could not direct them without reservation to any translation that I knew and trusted, so the idea of my own version took root.

Another reason I felt it was time for a new version was my frustration at seeing faulty religious ideas, specifically about the teachings of Jesus, dragging down important political advances in our society. You do not have to look far beneath the headlines to see uninformed, emotional, and sentimental notions of Jesus's philosophy. Today we cannot afford to keep referring to outmoded and faulty versions of Jesus's teachings and using them to support questionable causes.

In the end, I wanted to make the Gospels accessible and attractive to all sorts of readers. I see no indication that Jesus intended to create a religion or a church. His purpose is clear: He wanted to raise human awareness and behavior to another level, where it would surpass its tendencies toward self-interest, xenophobia, greed, religious moralism, and an emphasis on insignificant rules. He imagined a more just and pleasurable world, a "kingdom of the sky." He was explicit in instructing his students to speak to everyone, not just members of some particular and chosen religious group.

In my translation there is no suggestion that readers should believe in anything, join an organization, or abandon their cherished religious and philosophical ideals. I see no reason why a Christian, an agnostic, a Buddhist, or even an atheist would not be charmed and inspired by the Gospels. Anyone can freely and without any worries read the Gospels and be enriched.

These texts are sacred not because they belong to a particular religion or spiritual tradition but because they offer a vision and a way of life that transcends the limits of reason and will. They show a figure in love with life and with a heart open to all sorts of people, but at the same time a figure constantly in tune with the Sky Father, that image of ultimate transcendence that provides an opening, a tear in the fabric of human consciousness, a doorway to the infinite and the eternal.

The Gospels are not just books of practical wisdom—how to live more effectively. They are also books of mysteries, assuming that to be fully human we have to open ourselves to the mysterious depth and height of the world that is our home.

Who Was Jesus?

It is a simple question, isn't it? Who was Jesus? But the debate over the historical Jesus has been raging for at least two centuries. There is not much factual material to go on, and though the Gospels often sound like biography or history, clearly they are largely stories told to evoke a religious milieu. Historically, they are full of contradictions and gaps and fantasy material. This does not make them worthless in themselves. On the contrary, they are marvelous, simply ingenious inventions for spiritual teaching, but as history they are unreliable, to say the least.

It appears that Jesus was born around 4 BCE, when Romans were occupying the Mediterranean area of Jesus's birth and travels. Herod the Great was king, having been installed by the Romans. Greek language and culture were strong in the area, and Egypt, with its colorful past and rich spiritual culture, was not far away. There is evidence of a temple to the Greek god Dionysus in Jesus's area, and yet he was also dealing daily with Jewish teachings, customs, and rules. The Gospels portray many verbal skirmishes between Jesus and leaders, religious and social, who spoke up for Jewish law and tradition.

Jesus taught in the synagogues and to some appeared to be the long-awaited Messiah, the anointed leader of a new Jewish order. Many events and sayings in the Gospels echo Hebrew Bible writings, suggesting a layer of Messiah in Jesus's words and actions. But this aspect also casts a shadow on Jesus's presence and work, leading to the notion that he was "king of the Jews" and therefore a threat to Roman, local, and religious authority. Jesus was executed somewhere around 30 BCE, perhaps in his early thirties.

It is often said that people who read the Gospels see in them the Jesus they want to see. Some understand him to be a religious reformer, some a social rebel, and some the founder of a religious tradition. He is sometimes described as a teacher of wisdom, a label that comes close to my own view but is not quite serious enough. I see him more as a social mystic, like a shaman who can heal and lead people to appreciate multiple layers of reality.

At his baptism, the sky opens and the Sky Father speaks favorably of him, essentially blessing him. For me, this is a key moment, because Jesus is forever talking about his Father in the Sky, calling on us to always live in relation to that transcendent realm as well as in the present moment where our goodwill and powers of healing are always needed.

Jesus also has a relationship to the dead, and his own death is always looming. So in the end we have a Jesus who, as shaman and mystic, speaks and acts from the plane of daily life, from the transcendent level of the Father, and in the realm of the dead. He offers more than lessons in practical wisdom. His is a profound mystical vision that combines social action, based on the principle of friendship and not just altruism, with an all-encompassing mystical awareness of timeless realities and sensibilities.

Some think that Jesus wanted to create a religion or a church. Some think he was often speaking about the afterlife. In my translation and commentary, I move in a different direction. I think he was trying to convince people to live in an entirely different way, reflecting basic values of love and community, instead of self-interest and conflict. He suggested keeping the highest ideals in mind, instead of merely trying to amass money and possessions. He spoke and acted contrary to moralistic laws and customs, and showed in his manner of living that friends and good company were worth more than pious activities. He told all his students to be healers and to help people rid themselves of compulsive behaviors. Above all, he suggested that we break down all the artificial boundaries set up between religions and cultures and live as though we were all brothers and sisters. "Who is my family?" (Matthew 12:48), he asks, and he points to the students and others gathered around him.

What Is a Gospel?

The story of Jesus's life and teachings was written down, after a fairly long period of oral storytelling, by many writers, each having a different purpose. We get the essentials of the story in Mark, strong references to Jewish tradition in Matthew, important elaboration of the stories and teachings in Luke, and a mystical dimension in John. By the fifth century CE, the church had made these four versions official. They are called "canonical," the only ones approved by the church at that time: Matthew, Mark, Luke, and John. These writings first appeared somewhere between 65 CE and 110 CE, at least thirty-five years after Jesus's death. The book of Mark was the oldest, and the writers of Matthew and Luke took some material from Mark.

So think about that—a teacher appears and dies, and decades later a few devotees write down some stories about his life and try to capture his teachings, based on what had been passed down by word of mouth. Besides problems with memory, the various stories, as we see in the canonical Gospels, conveyed a different sense of what Jesus was all about. They were interpretations, not histories.

Two millennia later, we try to make sense of these written documents. Not being historians, we tend to take the stories as fact and even try to live by our interpretations. Some of the tales are quite fantastic: miraculous healings, raising the dead to life, the teacher himself surviving death, miraculous meals, and angels appearing here and there. Put together these two aspects—fantastic events and a tendency to take every word literally—and you have problems in understanding.

Strictly speaking, the word "Gospel" in the original Greek means "good message." It has been translated as "good news" or "glad tidings," both accurate and beautiful phrases. But what is the good news? That is not so easy to figure out.

The Translation

If you have grown up reading the Gospels or hearing them read in church, you may think that the translation you take for granted is official or sacred. But the Gospels were originally written in a form of Greek spoken by people in everyday life. Historians generally agree that Jesus spoke Aramaic and that the Gospels were written in Greek. There is no widely accepted ancient Aramaic version, though some think that the Greek Gospels, in particular Matthew and Luke, may have been based on Aramaic sources.

If you were to read the Gospels in the original Greek, you would be surprised, maybe even shocked, to see how simple the language is. The vocabulary is limited, and many sentences read almost like a book meant for children. The Book of Luke is somewhat more sophisticated than Mark, and Matthew lies in the middle. But, still, the Greek is quite plain. This means that a translator has great liberty in using a number of different words for the simple ones that keep coming up and is likely to infuse his version with his own biases and points of view.

In rendering the Greek Gospels into English, I would like to have come up with astonishing, florid, and entrancing phrases. But, as I said, the original is so simple that it would be a travesty to make it too elaborate. I had two principles in mind as I made this translation: I wanted to give the reader a version that would flow gracefully and be as clear and limpid as I could make it, and I wanted to use striking new English words for a few key terms that I thought were usually misunderstood.[1] I worked hard to be sure that my versions of these words had the backing of history and scholarship.

Jesus as Poet

I see Jesus as a spiritual poet. There is a striking passage in the Book of Matthew where his students are being literal and he corrects them. Matthew comments, "He said nothing to the people that was not a parable" (Matthew 13:34). By "poet" I do not mean that he speaks or writes poetry, but that he uses narrative and imagery to get his rich ideas across. He does not speak like an academic or a theologian, defining his terms and setting out his ideas pedantically. He is part teacher and part entertainer, a spiritual leader and a bard, a shaman and an enchanter.

A spiritual poet uses language for its beauty and for the power of its imagery. He wants to give the listener or reader insight into life. A poet does not force an understanding of life or an ideology onto his listeners. His narratives and images are meant to deepen a person's view of life. Some topics disappear in highly rationalistic language, while a more imagistic approach better conveys the mysteries involved.

If Jesus says that he speaks in parables, we should have a good idea about what a parable is. People often think of a parable as a simple teaching story with a moral. But scripture scholar Robert Funk says that a parable helps us "cross over" into the mysterious land that Jesus is trying to evoke for us, a kingdom in which life is radically different. Similarly, the renowned scholar John Dominic Crossan says that a parable "shatters our complacency" and pulls us out of the comfortable picture of life we have always lived by.

A parable is the opposite of a gentle teaching story. It confronts us, asking us to change our way of seeing things. It turns conventional ideas upside down. Its very point is to make us uncomfortable. In the Book of Matthew, Jesus says, "Love your enemies and speak well of those who criticize you. This way you can become sons of your Father in the Sky. For he makes the sun rise on the bad and the good and rain on the just and the unjust" (5:44–45).

For many, this teaching is just too radical. How many people show any love for those they consider enemies? Later he tells the parable of a woman who hid a small amount of yeast in a large pile of flour. That is what the Jesus kingdom is like. It is not overt, not even visible, and it is tiny. Yet it can change a life and alter the course of the world. If only a small portion of people in the world understood that somehow you have to love your enemies, we might not go on dividing ourselves into the good and the bad, and the Jesus vision would gain some traction.

Much of what is written in the Gospels is poetic in style, sometimes metaphorical and allegorical. You have to have a sharp and sophisticated appreciation for symbol and image or you might completely misread the text.

For example, Jesus heals a blind man. Is this a simple miraculous good deed or does it speak to a less literal blindness? Do we all fail to see life for what it is and have the wrong view of our place in the world? The Gospel writer himself speaks about this more poetic kind of blindness.

A Better Word for "Sin"

Many translations of the Gospels have a moralistic air. The translator may think of Christianity as a religion of do's and don'ts, and that point of view leads him to translate certain words with a heavy moral slant. Take the word "sin," so often used in English versions. Many readers of the Gospels know that the word originally meant "off the mark." Yet we do not use the word "sin" that way. We mean that someone has done something so bad that it merits everlasting punishment.

As a child growing up in a devout Catholic family, I was always being told, "Don't do that. You'll go to hell." What if an adult had said to me, "There you go again. You're off the mark. You need to get your values straight." At least I would have had a chance to do better.

I do not translate the Greek word *hamartia* as "sin" or even "off the mark." I prefer the reflections of the pre-Christian philosopher Aristotle, who in his book on poetry and drama, *Poetics*, discusses the role of *hamartia* in tragedy. He says it refers to an action done out of ignorance that has tragic consequences.

When I was a child, I had a BB gun and shot some birds. I still feel remorse for doing such a thing. I needed to be taught the value of innocent animal life. My ignorance led me to actions I now regret. I would not say that I committed a sin, but that in my ignorance I made a mistake that today I mourn. I do not consider myself a horrible person and carry that guilt with me, but I understand that I have to keep learning and become more aware so I do not make worse mistakes.

With Aristotle's thoughtful explanation in mind, how would you translate *hamartia*? It is complicated. Maybe several words would be better than one. I tend to use the word "mistake," but I know that alone it sounds too weak. Usually I qualify it according to the context in which it is used. I do not want to imply that *hamartia* is a simple, everyday misstep, but neither do I want to suggest high-minded moralistic judgment, which I do not pick up from the Gospels in Greek. So I often used the phrase "tragic mistake" in this series.

I have seen many English translations of the Gospels that try to make the language more modern in style than the familiar, often archaic renditions. I appreciate many of these modern versions, but none interprets the Gospels the way I do. I have my own idea of what the Gospels are about, and my translation expresses that viewpoint. "Sin" is only one of many key words that affect the way we understand what Jesus was up to and what he taught. Not finding "sin" in this translation, I hope you read the Gospels without beating yourself up for having done wrong. I hope you see that Jesus was not moralistic but rather deeply concerned about the roots of self-serving and destructive behavior.

Some Key Images

For years, in writing many books, I have turned to Greek classical literature for insight, especially the great tragedies and comedies, the hymns to the gods and goddesses, and the mythological stories. In the Gospel translation, whenever I come across any connection between the Gospels and these classical sources I take note of the crossover and see if it offers any special insight. In some cases, the parallels are striking and in others subtle and hidden. In general, an aware-ness of earlier uses of Greek terms helps us understand better what is being said in the Gospels.

As a student of both religion and depth psychology, I have spent many years studying Greek polytheism. I have been amazed by the richness, com-plexity, and insightfulness of the ancient tales of the gods and goddesses. If you were to read some of the penetrating essays by my mentor James Hill-man or the well-known mythologist Joseph Campbell, you would see how the old Greek stories help us gain insight into the patterns and dynamics of our everyday lives.

As I was poring over the Greek text of the Gospels, studying one key word after another, I discovered several instances in which a reference to one of the ancient Greek stories lay buried in the etymology or structure of the word.

The Kingdom of the Sky

The clearest example is the phrase "kingdom of heaven" or "our Father who art in heaven." The Greek word usually translated as "heaven" is *ouranos*. The word could be taken as an ordinary term for the sky, but it is also the exact name for the sky-god of the Greeks, Ouranos, today usually spelled Uranus, like the planet.

When I read the words "kingdom of heaven" (*ouranos*), I am inclined to translate it as "kingdom of the sky." I will say more about this image later, but my point here is that the Greek version of the Gospels has layers, and, whether intended or not, deep themes peek through and enrich the stories and teachings.

The Kingdom

You get the sense in the Gospels that Jesus is an intimate and special son of the Sky Father. The kingdom he is creating on earth is a way of life sanctioned by this father. When asked how to pray, Jesus says, "Say, our Father in the Sky, may your name be held sacred. . . ."

I see the sky as a metaphor, or better yet, an archetypal image. Its meaning is based on ordinary experience: You look at the sky at night or even during the day, and you may wonder about the meaning of everything and your place in life. You may imagine other worlds, other planets, and other civilizations. You may look into the light-blue daytime heavens or the blue-black night and sense infinity and eternity. The kingdom of the sky, therefore, is not like practical, pedestrian, and self-absorbed life. It is an alternative, the object of wonder and perfection, eternal and infinite. The "Father" of that realm offers a more perfected idea of what human life could be.

The kingdom of the sky comprises those people who live the values Jesus specifies in his teaching, especially the one about respecting any person who is not of your circle. Jesus does not talk about love as a sentimental emotion. That is why I usually translate *agape* as "respect." If your basic motivation in all of life is love and respect, you are automatically in the kingdom. But take note: Jesus makes it clear that your actions have to follow your values in this regard.

The Sky and the Sky Father

I prefer to use the word "sky" instead of "heaven" because it is a concrete image. I do not mean a literal father in the clouds but rather the sky as an image for spirit. As I have read the passages about the Sky Father, I have had in mind the Native American mystic Black Elk, praying to the parents and grandparents in the sky.

Here is a typical passage from Black Elk that influenced me in translating
Ouranos:

The fifth Grandfather spoke, the oldest of them all, the Spirit of the
Sky. "My boy," he said, "I have sent for you and you have come. My
power you shall see!" He stretched his arms and turned into a spotted eagle hovering. "Behold," he said, "all the wings of the air shall
come to you, and they and the winds and the stars shall be like relatives. You shall go across the earth with my power." Then the eagle
soared above my head and fluttered there; and suddenly the sky was
full of friendly wings all coming toward me.[2]

This passage has much in common with the Gospels, as when Jesus is baptized
and the Father speaks from the sky and the spirit appears as a hovering dove. The
Gospel describes the sky as sometimes full of not wings but angels—close by.

Hesiod, one of the early Greek spiritual poets, describes *ouranos*—the word
used every time for Gospel phrases like "kingdom of the sky" and "our father in
the heavens"—this way:

The first one born of Gaia (Earth) was Ouranos.
He was as big as she was.
He was the sky full of stars.
He spread over her
and was
a solid ground for the holy immortals.

You can pray to the Father, as Jesus did, and yet know that you are address-
ing something mysterious and vastly spiritual. Our usual anthropomorphic—
human-like—language is only an approximation of the sublime mystery of this
Father. As the spirit of the sky, he is the "ground for the holy immortals" or, we
might say, "the ground for our spiritual vision."

The kingdom of the sky, or the heavens, is a place set apart because of
its special values and the primacy of its rule of love and respect, *agape*. Jesus
endorses neither the rule-bound religion of the church officials nor the self-
satisfied realm of the purely secular. He calls for a third alternative, a place
where you can live a life based on spiritual values of love and respect.

The Commentary

Because there are so many words of such complexity in the Gospels, I have included many notes on the translation and comments on the meaning. Some of these comments come from other sources, offering either an expert reflection on the passage or special insight from an artist. From the beginning I wanted to include comments from thinkers of many different fields and spiritual traditions. Why not? Their different perspectives open up fresh ways of understanding the Gospel stories and teachings. I try to set aside my own academic interests and get to the heart of the matter. If I mention an expert or a writer from history, like Aristotle's thoughts about mistakes, or a poet like Anne Sexton, I do not call on them as authorities, as though I were writing a school paper. I mention them because their brilliant ideas are relevant. I hope that their way of seeing the issue will enrich your reading of the Gospels.

Most of the time my comments are my own take on the passage in question. A friend advised me on this project: "People aren't going to read your version because you're a scholar or have a mind-blowing translation to offer. They'll want to know what you think about the various stories and teachings. They want to know your ideas because you write about the soul and how to live more deeply and with less conflict." I took what he said to heart and beefed up my own commentary.

I want to open up the Gospel message by showing how people of various traditions and expertise interpreted certain passages. I quote Christian, Jewish, Sufi, Buddhist, and secular writers; poets, politicians, theologians, and Bible experts. Then I bring my own point of view to various passages, basing my reflections on my studies in depth psychology, world religions, mythology, and the arts. I rely on decades of experience as a psychotherapist, and I am aware of my own development in relation to the Gospels, from my childhood, when I heard them naively; to my monastic days, when I studied them in a Christian context; to now, when I blend the sacred and secular in everything I do and when I am always the psychotherapist. I could make a case that Jesus was a psychotherapist, and, in fact, the word "therapy" is often used in the Greek version to denote Jesus as a healer.

I think that the deeper point of the Gospels has been lost over the years, when people have focused on them as a source of strict moral lessons and the cornerstones for belief, and the establishment of a religion, church, or spiritual community. To me, Jesus says clearly that he is speaking to everyone who will listen, and his message has sophisticated psychological insight. My intention with the commentary is to release the Gospels from their narrow confinements and show how valuable they are today to anyone at all looking for insight into how to live deeply and lovingly.

The Gospels Are for Everyone

Returning to a close study of the Gospels has helped me personally with my spiritual life. These texts now inspire me more forcefully than at any time in my life. I do not see them as representing or advocating a particular religious viewpoint but as setting out a way of life, a secular set of values, that could help humanity survive and thrive. While I certainly do not want to convert anyone to a particular religion or church, I would like to see the whole world adopt this vision for humanity, based on love, respect, healing, and compassion.

I hope this new translation will move us in a more thoughtful, subtle, and compassionate direction in our own way of living and in our attitude toward others, especially those different from us. This is a key part of Jesus's teachings: He is forever telling people to love those who are outside their own circle. The kingdom is for them, he says, not for the in crowd.

My own practice is to refer to several different translations of sacred texts. I have seven versions of the Tao Te Ching on my shelves close at hand. I recommend doing the same with the Gospels. For example, I have relied on the beautiful translation by the Jesus Seminar in a book called *The Acts of Jesus*. I respect the scholarship behind that translation, though I did not want to use such complicated language in my own version. I admire the witty and profound translations of certain passages by John Dominic Crossan in his book *The Essential Jesus*. "The somebodies will be nobodies and the nobodies will be somebodies." You cannot get a better translation than that.

If you are looking for a more extravagant version or something completely different, those translations are available. But if you want an accurate version that is close to the original in vocabulary and tone, presented in simple, rhythmic English, then mine might do. If you want help understanding the sometimes difficult passages, not from a scholar's point of view but from someone with a background in depth psychology, literature, and world religions, then you may want to add this one to your collection.

It is my conviction that the less literally you take most passages, the more you will be inspired to live an altogether different kind of life, one in which your heart is more open than you ever thought it could be. You will have found a kind of utopia, an island of meaning radically different from the one that rules the world today. You can live this way now and find joy and substance in your life. And you can promote it as a way for the future—not a belief system or a church or religion, but a way of being in the world, open and radically accepting.

Introduction to the Book of Luke

The Book of Luke is the work of an artist, a person sensitive to the craft of storytelling and able to provide details that add interest and clarity. Accordingly, this Gospel is the longest of the four canonical Gospels; it is twice as long as Mark. But it is a joy to read because it has novelistic elements of style. One example would be the infancy narratives, elaborate and charming stories surrounding the conception and birth of Jesus. But other stories, too, are full of details that make it easy to imagine the events described.

If you look at paintings inspired by the Gospel stories, you see many details that are usually left out of the written narratives. For example, many paintings of the annunciation show Mary with a book in her lap that may hint at the passages in the Hebrew Bible preparing for this event or Mary's thoughtfulness and devotion. The book may teach that study is good preparation for inspiration and revelation.

The artist Luke gives many details that other versions of the stories leave out. A simple example: Both Matthew and Luke recount the parable of the lost sheep, in which a shepherd is happy to have found just one out of a flock of ninety-nine. Luke adds the details that the shepherd put the sheep up on his shoulders and then called his friends and neighbors together to celebrate.

Luke has been called a painter, a photographer, and even a detective, writing as though he were present in the stories he tells, even though he says at the outset that he based his narrative on the eyewitness accounts of others. The point is not to ask whether Luke was present historically but to notice that he is a skillful narrator, quoting statements and taking the viewpoint of the omniscient author, writing as though he were indeed present and taking notes.

Luke prefaces the parable of the lost sheep with the scene of the Pharisees complaining about Jesus eating with tax collectors, usually seen as corrupt, and people lost and acting out. So we can understand the story as part of Jesus's notion of a new kingdom, a different world, in which people who are confused can find their way. This is the essence of Jesus's teaching, and Luke's details of holding the sheep and celebrating with friends hint at Jesus's warm attention to people who are lost. He is, in fact, a good shepherd because of his heartfelt dedication to those who are lost. Oftentimes, people who feel chosen and righteous are not open to the deep change and radical communal sense that Jesus's kingdom calls for.

Jesus at Dinner

Another detail in the previous story not to be overlooked is that Jesus is dining with people not exactly approved by the religious authorities. While this special theme—eating, dining together—is strong in the Gospels as a whole, it is more so in Luke.

There are as many as fifty references to food in Luke. They provide a basic metaphor for life in the kingdom, and that metaphor is not a simple one. Food has many different meanings, all of them connected to the central image of Jesus and his mission.

One of the key issues raised by these stories of food and eating together, discussed by several New Testament scholars and anthropologists, is discerning who sits at your table. The religious leaders criticize Jesus for reclining at dinner with people usually considered unfit, whether it is a tax collector or a woman with a bad reputation. But he also eats with friends and relatives, culminating in the Last Supper, a ritual meal with his closest companions. Luke also adds the mysterious story of the meal at Emmaus, in which his followers recognize Jesus as he breaks bread.

One of Jesus's primary concerns is to create a more radical sense of community, in which people normally considered strangers or even enemies would now care for each other. Those people may sit at our table who would ordinarily be considered another class, race, nationality, religion, or political group. Obviously, in our otherwise sophisticated world, we have not yet achieved this kind of communal sensibility.

The highly respected New Testament scholar John Dominic Crossan uses a word from anthropology for this radical kind of community—"commensality." *Com* means together and *mensa* means table. Crossan describes it as "a shared egalitarianism of spiritual and material resources." He uses a dramatic image for what he is talking about: "It concerns the longest journey in the Greco-Roman world, maybe in any world, the step across the threshold of a peasant stranger's home."[1]

Jesus's teaching and example ask that we become seriously more inclusive of who we consider our neighbor, and this shift toward radical community is at the heart of his message. In the Gospels, and especially in Luke, we find it in the form of eating together, sharing a meal, and all the hospitality and conversation that go with dining.

Another way of reading the many references to food and dining in Luke is one I have not found explicit in scholarly writings: the Epicurean aspect of eating. Epicurus was a Greek philosopher known mainly for his philosophy of pleasure. Over the centuries he has been misunderstood, and his name has been used for an excess of pleasure, hedonism, that was not his idea. He advocated deep ordinary pleasures, such as friendship and intimate community. He taught a small group in Athens in a garden and included many different kinds of people. In many ways, the image of Jesus in the Gospels echoes the portrait of Epicurus himself.

Jesus's clear enjoyment of the pleasures of dining and being with friends and living a modest but pleasurable life sets him apart from the many religious people who instead emphasize rules, the suppression of appetites, and a life of deprivation. Jesus's kingdom is one of joy and even moderate sensuality. His deeply human and moderate ways represent just one of many qualities he shares with effortless Taoism and the Middle Way of the Buddha.

Perhaps the most sensuous moment is when a woman with an alabaster jar of ointment approaches Jesus and rubs his feet with the oil. Matthew and Mark describe the scene briefly and then go on to criticize the action. But Luke offers far more detail: "She brought an alabaster jar full of perfume. She placed herself behind him at his feet and cried and wet his feet with her tears, wiping them with her hair, and she kissed his feet and rubbed them with fragrant oil." Then Jesus goes over the scene in detail, telling his host exactly what just happened. And remember, all this happened in the context of a dinner.

Luke's artistic style, his tendency to include small physical details, and his interest in the body and in food come together to show Jesus as a human being tolerant of human weakness and far less judgmental than the religious leaders around him. This is an Epicurean Jesus who loves life and people and takes opportunities for sensuous joy in everyday life.

An Epicurean approach to life, as I am describing it, is a route to soul in everyday life and therefore would offer a soul-centered way of following through on Jesus's teaching and example. It has soul because it brings into play our deepest common humanity. We do not see our differences as obstacles but rather as sources of enrichment. We understand that we are all diners on this planet, enjoying the taste of food and the quality of conversation. These simple pleasures are more important than they may seem to be. They can be the force that holds humanity together, when other forces push us apart.

Women in Luke

Another important aspect of Luke's Gospel, noted by many close readers, is the significant role of women throughout the Gospel. In Matthew, an angel appears in a dream to Joseph offering advice. In Luke, an angel appears to Mary announcing her special destiny. The long story is told of Elizabeth and the birth of her son John, and in that story, Mary recites what has come to be known as the Magnificat, a poem of praise in which she says, "My soul magnifies the Lord."

Luke tells many stories about women—Mary and Martha, the women at the cross, women healed, parables that feature women. Some scholars even wonder if Luke was a woman, a possibility I think worth considering. It is not just that he includes many women in his cast of characters, but he also demonstrates a degree of sensitivity we could easily associate with a woman author/editor. Of course, a man can be sensitive, but since this quality stands out in Luke, it might be worth entertaining the possibility of a woman evangelist.

In the story of the crucifixion and burial of Jesus, Luke also gives a prominent role to the women who were with Jesus in Galilee. These were obviously devoted followers who appear to be closer to Jesus in his last hour than the men. Luke names them as Mary of Magdala, Joanna, and Mary the mother of James, and he mentions that there were other women as well. They were near the execution place; they checked out the tomb, prepared ointments, and found the empty tomb. They reported all this to the eleven apostles, who did not believe the women.

These women also saw the two figures standing at the empty tomb, the ones whose clothing flashed like lightning. All four Gospels tell of these two; Matthew calls them angels. Mark adds Salome to the two Marys who witness the events at the tomb. All together we get the impression that the women have the privilege of being close to the remarkable events of the burial and resurrection.

Some feminist readers point out that even though Luke gives women a prominent role, they are not granted a position of leadership. And men still have trouble seeing women as equals. At least we can appreciate a strong feminine presence in the last crucial phases of Jesus's mission to the world and take note of their role in the story of being mediators between the brilliant realm above and the confused and fearful male students cooped up in a room.

Throughout history the Gospels have been read with male eyes, giving a biased angle on many of the events. Today we have strong voices and a fresh appreciation of the Gospels coming from many insightful women who have come to the foreground of New Testament scholarship.

Engaging the Imagination

Scholars tell us that Luke used Mark as one of his sources, but Luke does not write like Mark, and so we find fresh versions of those stories. For example, Mark tells the story of Levi, the tax collector, in sparse terms: "As he was walking along, he saw Levi, son of Alphaeus, sitting at the revenue booth. 'Join me,' Jesus said, and the man got up and followed him." In Luke we have the memorable and charming detail of Zaccheus, a short man, climbing a tree to see Jesus over the heads of the crowd. Then Jesus invites him to come down and offers him dinner.

This detail of the tree is full of meaning: How important it is to "see" Jesus, to have a real encounter, to get over the intellectual and moral blindness we encounter often in the Gospels, and to recognize how small we all are, in need of help so we can rise above the crowd.

Scholars also say that Luke used the Q source, the theoretical written record of sayings and events that many experts believe was used by the Gospel writers to create their highly theological tales about Jesus and his teachings. The experts also say that Luke used an L source, Luke's own material that gives his Gospel its particular flavor and value.

Some contemporary readers could say that there is also an R source for all the Gospels, the reader. You and me. We bring many assumptions and biases to our reading. We are also many readers at once. I catch myself reading like the six-year-old who understood it all literally and naively. I try to nudge him away and let a more sophisticated reader take over.

Because Luke engages our imaginations with the concrete, sensuous details in his stories, we are even more involved as active readers. I do not mean that we are interpreting in our own ways, an issue much in dispute over the centuries, but that as we read we picture the scenes in our minds so that they come alive for us. We may add our own minor details, making the stories our own.

Translating Luke

I have chosen a challenging task in this volume. I want to present a fresh wording of the text so that the reader will be stopped and provoked to think. I do not use words such as "sin" and "heaven," which have become routine and expected. My translation and commentary may startle, but I believe that startle, shock, and surprise are valuable ways to come to life spiritually and intellectually. Besides, I think my choice of words is more accurate than the familiar ones. Why else have a new translation?

I consciously decided not to offer a colloquial, loose translation but simply to allow the English words to flow rhythmically, to read more gracefully. By carefully changing key words and phrases, such as using "Lord of earth and sky" instead of "heaven," over the course of reading the whole Gospel, you may have a radically different understanding of what the Gospels are all about. For instance, you may sense that, instead of taking you out of this world, they place you in the deepest part of yourself and your life.

Since Luke used Mark's Gospel, obviously he wrote later, some say around 85 CE or even into the next century. To complicate things, many experts believe that Luke was also the author of the Acts of the Apostles, and they often refer to Luke-Acts as a single composition.

Because he is skillful at telling a story, I assume that Luke is subtle and understands the place of hidden, layered, and even clever words and details. I think that most people read the Gospels without that appreciation of art and poetic devices and therefore misread or miss the message.

An example would be Luke's story of the prodigal son, not found in the other Gospels, where a young man squanders his inheritance on a wild life. His father says later that he was lost and is now found, was dead and is now alive. The Greek word here for "dead" is *nekron*, the same word Matthew uses in his Gospel when Jesus sends his students out "to raise the dead," as most translations say. But Luke's story might help us broaden our idea about raising the dead. Maybe the point is to recover those who are lost and make those who have been acting out unconsciously embrace a meaningful life, like the prodigal son. I prefer to change "raising the dead" to "waking up the unconscious," a more accurate translation.

Expanding the Breadth and Depth of Love

It helps to have a good commentary or to read books on the Gospels, but you have to be discerning. Many are dogmatic and tell you what to believe, or moralistic and tell you how to behave. As I read the Gospels, I see their purpose as to inspire us to a new level of existence and to a way of life based on love and neighborliness. Commentators will point out that Luke's interest in making Jesus's teachings available to people of all kinds comes through in his genealogy, which starts not with Abraham, the Jewish line, but with Adam, the first human.

A neighbor is not someone who is part of your club or family, but someone who lives in your vicinity or on your planet, and who may be entirely different from you in his thinking and style. This is how I understand Jesus when he looks at the people around him and says, "You are my mother and my brothers" (Luke 8:21). His message is for the people of the world, not those who make up his inner circle.

Only Luke tells the stories of the prodigal son and the good Samaritan, both about the unreasonable lengths love must take us. For love's sake we do what is illogical and break unnecessary rules. Jesus does not preach conventional, simple behavior. He recommends a radically different way of life that goes against common sense and ordinary ideas of propriety. He does not want to make life somewhat better or help you feel virtuous. He wants to transform the world. In Luke these themes are especially strong and appear as compassion, forgiveness, and inclusive community.

Jesus has a utopian message. He envisions an ideal world where love is absolute and forgiveness routine. It is a world not yet fully implemented, but is found today only in certain places or moments. The empty tomb allows us to imagine that he is now present in a different form, perhaps as his teaching goes out into the world to inspire a more peaceful existence. His kingdom is approaching, but is not yet settled in.

Luke addresses his book to Theophilus. Is that a person who was his companion or in his circle? The name means "God lover." So maybe Luke is speaking to anyone capable of a love that extends beyond reason and convention, that can be the energy enlivening the human soul and the cosmos.

Everywhere—Jesus

The Book of Luke ends with two stories of great importance for our understanding of Jesus and his teaching. In the first story, two followers are walking on the road to Emmaus and bump into Jesus. They have a meal together, and just when Jesus breaks bread they recognize him. This story may echo a ritual meal in the early days of the Jesus movement, but it also picks up the theme of Jesus as spiritual food and the fact that, as the embodiment of his vision, he can be found in everyday life, not just in explicitly religious contexts.

In the other story, Jesus goes up into the sky. He is now no longer an ordinary person but a sky being. He is a spiritual presence through his teaching, his modeling of a utopian life and the law of love. We get it wrong when we focus only on believing the teachings or being a member of some religious organization. Jesus is now found in the image of the sky—our ideals, our vision for humanity, our universal love for all beings.

The Gospel of Thomas has a line that states this mystical insight quite plainly: "Split a piece of wood. I am there" (77b). The message at Emmaus was this: Break bread and you will see me. In this, the Gospel is close to the Tao Te Ching, which says:

> *The human is inspired by the Earth,*
> *Earth is inspired by the Sky,*
> *The Sky is inspired by the Tao,*
> *The Tao is inspired by what is. (verse 25)*

There is a chain from ordinary life to the sky (often mentioned in the Gospels) and the Jesus teaching, his version of the Tao. The Tao Te Ching also says, "The

Tao is the source of the Ten Thousand Things" (verse 62). Translated another way, it says, "The Tao is that toward which all things flow."

Jesus's teaching reveals the law of life. It is not an arbitrary teaching, the vision of one person. It is an unveiling of what is, how life flows, and how to return to your natural, original state of being and enjoy abundant life. With his choice of stories and his rich way of telling them, Luke shows with remarkable clarity who and what Jesus was and inspires his readers to follow his way as a route to the very heart of existence.

THE BOOK OF
LUKE

1   Luke offers a brief preface to his Gospel, assuring his readers that he is using reliable sources, he has done a deep study of them, and he has made his own "careful account." He addresses this preface to Theophilus, maybe a real person or maybe the reader. The name Theophilus means "God-lover." He may be speaking to anyone who loves God, which can imply a reader who lives a transcendent life and is open to the mysterious world in which he or she lives.

2   The story of Elizabeth and Zechariah not only connects Jesus to Jewish tradition, but it also psychologically places the story of Jesus in a spiritual context. Angels and healings and miracles, trust and faithfulness, appear at the very beginning of the Gospel. These are the themes Jesus emphasizes in his teachings. It deepens the connection between him and John, who baptized him. John is like an alter ego, an echo figure, giving dimension to the plot of Jesus's life.

Chapter 1

Many have tried their hand at telling an accurate story about the events that played out here among us. We received the details from some who were eyewitnesses and keepers of the story, and after examining these materials at length, I would like to give you, my noble Theophilus, a careful account. I'd like you to have a trustworthy version of these events that you have studied.[1]

Herod was king of Judea at the time when Zechariah, of the sacerdotal section of Abijah, fulfilled his duty as priest. His wife Elizabeth was a descendant of Aaron. Both were sterling followers of the commandments and laws and were spotless in the sight of God. But they had no children. Elizabeth was physically incapable and they were both well on in years.[2]

Zechariah's team was on call, and so he was an acting priest in the presence of God. It was customary in those days to select someone by lot to enter the Lord's temple and burn incense. When it was time to light the incense, the worshippers gathered outdoors to pray. At that moment, Zechariah had a vision of an angel, the Lord's messenger, standing to the right of the incense altar. Seeing the angel, Zechariah was astonished and began to panic. But the angel spoke to him, "Don't be afraid, Zechariah. Your prayer has been answered. Your wife Elizabeth will have a baby, a son, and you should call him John.

3 Not only does John prepare the community for the appearance of Jesus, but he also plays an important part in the Gospel story by offering a context for Jesus's work and teaching. He will open hearts and soften cynicism.

4 Zechariah stands in clear contrast to Mary, who, when Gabriel visits her later, does not hesitate to go along with the invitation to a special life (Luke 1:38). Zechariah's punishment, loss of speech, seems appropriate. Later, Jesus will cure many who cannot speak, suggesting, as in the parable, that in the kingdom, people have a strong voice, speaking for the values of that special level of existence.

5 Gabriel, whose name means "God's strength," is a major figure in the spiritual realm. He is an agent of the Divine who helps Daniel understand a dream and later appears to Muhammad with a text to read, leading the Prophet to embark on his mission. Muhammad refers to Gabriel as being between heaven and earth, a good description of the role of a major angel. Gabriel also appears in the Book of Enoch.

"You'll find joy and happiness with him, and many people will gladly celebrate his birth and he will be special in the eye of the Lord. He will never drink wine or stronger drinks and from the time he's in his mother's body a holy spirit will fill him. He'll convert many of Israel's children to the Lord their God. He'll have the spirit and charisma of Elijah and be close to God. He'll open the hearts of parents so that they're warm to their children. He'll soften the cynical so they'll be compassionate. He'll get people ready for the Lord."[3]

Zechariah asked the angel, "Is there some way I can be sure of this? After all, I'm an old man and my wife is getting on."

The angel responded, "I am Gabriel. I stand in the presence of God and was sent to speak with you and give you this good news. Now, because you didn't trust what I said, you won't be able to talk until the day it all takes place. In due time, it will all come true."[4]

All this time the people were wondering what was going on with Zechariah and waiting for him to exit the sanctuary. When he finally appeared, he couldn't speak, and they realized that he had had a vision while in the sanctuary. He made gestures, but was still not able to talk. When his period of service was over, he went back home.

Later, his wife Elizabeth became pregnant and for five months remained in seclusion. She told people, "The Lord looked on me with pleasure and did this for me and removed any embarrassment I may have felt among people."

In the sixth month God sent the angel Gabriel[5] to a town in Galilee called Nazareth to a young woman engaged to a man named Joseph, from the house of David. Her name was Mary. The angel drew near and said,

"Hello, grace-filled one, the Lord is with you."

His words confused her and she wondered what they could mean.

6   "'Overshadow'—a verb that explicitly picks up the mysterious image that closes the Book of Exodus, when the *shekinah*, the cloud that is the spirit of God, covers the Ark of the Covenant. . . . Just as God was present at the Ark of the Old Covenant, so he covers the Ark of the New."
    —Maria Warner, *Alone of All Her Sex: The Myth and the Cult of the Virgin Mary* (New York: Alfred A. Knopf, 1976), 11

This story echoes the Greek tale of Danae, a woman shut up in a bronze chamber so she would not get pregnant with a son who would threaten his father. The great Zeus, however, came to her in the form of a rain shower and made her pregnant with the hero Perseus.

7   I consider these three words among the most important in the Gospels: "Let it be." In the face of profound mystery and a challenge to Mary's entire existence, she bows in submission to a divine decree. Many times, in an ordinary life, each of us may face the demands of fate. We are challenged to enter into our own destiny. Mary is our exemplar, as she says, "Let it be."

The angel said to her,

"Don't be afraid, Mary. God is pleased with you. You will conceive and have a son you will call Jesus. He will be magnificent and will be honored as the son of the very highest, and the Lord God will give him the throne of his ancestor David. He will rule the house of Jacob forever and his kingdom will never end."

Mary answered the angel, "How can this be? I've never known a man."

The angel said to her,

> *"A holy spirit will come over you*
> *and the power of the highest will envelop you in shadow*[6]
> *and the holy being to be born*
> *will be called a son of God.*

"Now, your relative Elizabeth, though old, is pregnant with a son and in her sixth month—she was thought to be infertile. With God nothing is impossible."

"Here I am, the Lord's servant. What you have said, let it be."[7]

The angel left.

8 This is a beautiful poem of praise for the source of life that has done wonders for this humble woman. The poem is known as "Magnificat," the opening word in Latin, and as "The Song of Mary." We could each write a poem to be our own "Magnificat," magnifying the life that makes us who we are.

9 This is a key theme in the later teaching of Jesus: The last will be first and the first last (Luke 13:30). A profound reversal or inversion takes place when a person surrenders to the power and life flowing through her that will make her who she is intended to be.

10 "The first half of v. 48 does point to Hannah, however, for it echoes her prayer in 1 Samuel 1:11. . . . Hannah is quite possibly the ideal mother of the Old Testament and is therefore a fit model for Mary. There are also echoes of another Old Testament mother, Leah. Leah is also an appropriate model for Mary for she is the mother of Judah. It is from Judah, the tribe, that the Messiah is to come. . . . Luke formed his own addition to a hymn that already existed."
  —Stephen Farris, *The Hymns of Luke's Infancy Narratives: Their Origins, Meaning and Significance* (Sheffield, England: JSOT Press, 1985), 25–26

Later Mary went out and hurried to a Judean hill town in the
countryside. There she went to Zechariah's home and greeted
Elizabeth. When Elizabeth heard Mary's good wishes, the
baby in her womb leaped, and Elizabeth was inspired with a
holy spirit and cried out, "Among women you are blessed, and
blessed is the fruit of your womb. Why would the mother of my
Lord come to me? What's special about me? As soon as I heard
your greeting, the baby in me leaped for joy. How blessed is
this woman who trusted what the Lord told her."

Mary chanted,

> *My soul magnifies the Lord,*[8]
> *And my spirit is very happy with my savior God.*
> *He has noticed the humility of his servant*
> *And from now on all people will think of me*
> *In bliss,*
> *That mighty power has accomplished*
> *Wonders for me.*
> *And his name is sacred.*
> *His kindness is for those who venerate him*
> *From one generation to another.*
> *He has used his arm with power*
> *And has sent scattering those*
> *Who are inappropriately proud.*
> *He has brought the powerful down*
> *From their high positions*
> *And lifted up the lowly.*[9]
> *He has satisfied those who are hungry*
> *And sent the wealthy away empty.*
> *Remembering his promise of mercy*
> *To our ancestors,*
> *To Abraham*
> *And to his children forever,*
> *He has been kind to Israel.*[10]

11 Finally, Zechariah speaks in accord with the divine will or the law of life. Doing so, he regains his own speech. Especially in the Gospel of John, Jesus teaches, almost speaking stereophonically—at the human level and at a much more exalted level—to be always at one with the Father in the Sky.

12 Praise is an important kind of prayer, here a blessing as well as an expression of gratitude. Today we may not stop to pray in this way or to offer a blessing on our friends and family members. Yet both help us live in the world spiritually, with an eye always open to the transcendent and timeless.

Mary stayed with Elizabeth for three months and then went home. When the time came for Elizabeth to have her baby, she gave birth to a son. Her neighbors and family knew that the Lord had shown her this special kindness and were happy for her.

On the eighth day people came to circumcise the baby. They were going to call him Zechariah, after his father, but his mother said, "No. He will be called John."

But they complained, "This name isn't in the family."

They signaled the father to get his opinion. He asked for something to write on and scribbled, "His name is John." Everyone was surprised. Then as soon as he opened his mouth he found his tongue freed, and he spoke, giving honor to God.[11]

The neighbors were frightened and the entire hill country of Judea talked about what had happened. People who heard the news wondered, "What's going to become of this child?" The hand of the Lord was upon him.

His father Zechariah was filled with a holy spirit and uttered this prophecy:

> *Praise to the Lord God of Israel*[12]
> *He looked caringly upon his people*
> *And rescued them.*
> *He made an altar of healing*
> *In the house of his servant David.*
> *He said this long ago*
> *Through the voices of his holy prophets.*
> *He saved us from our adversaries*
> *And from the hands of those who despise us.*
> *He acted kindly for our fathers*
> *And kept his promise,*
> *The vow he made to our father Abraham*
> *To protect us from our enemies*

13 It is good to remember, especially in challenging times, the "tender mercies" that life offers us. We may not feel cared for by the forces of life, and that absence of care may come from our failure to recognize tender mercies when they come along. A poem of praise would help us remember who we are and what kind of world we live in. In spite of all the tragedies around us, life still offers beauty, pleasure, and the possibility of love.

14 Here we find an early version of a central theme in the Gospels: Forgiveness is a path to healing. Not only forgiving others and ourselves, but also simply reaching a point where we feel absolved for the wrongs we have done.

So we could serve him without being afraid
With holiness and compassion
In his presence as long as we live.
You, child, will be known as the
Prophet of the highest one.
You will go ahead of the Lord
To prepare his paths.
He will let his people know
How to be healed
Through having their faults forgiven
Through the tender mercies of our God[13]
And dawn in the sky breaking out on us
Illuminating those who crouch down in darkness
And the shadow of death
Guiding our steps on the path of peace.[14]

The child grew up and matured spiritually and stayed in the wilderness until he presented himself in public to Israel.

1 There is some disagreement about whether it was an inn or a guest room that was not available; I translate this as "hotel," assuming an inn can be a hotel. What is important is that the baby honored by an army of angels was born in a lowly place.

2 As the psychoanalysts Carl Jung and Otto Rank have pointed out, it is a common theme to see the hero as an infant abandoned and left exposed and in danger. In Jung's view, anything new, any promising beginning, is in a fragile condition and needs special care and protection.

   There never was room in civil or religious society for Jesus. He was a wanderer or saunterer. It seems true, as well, that any of us who appreciate the gospel teaching, live a life of radical compassion, and embrace healing as our life work will not have a home in society and often not even in religious communities. Because of our vision, because of our interpretation of the Jesus kingdom, we are wayfarers.

3 Notice that angels often say, "Don't be afraid." Fear can keep you from enjoying the great satisfactions of life. A spiritual life requires courage and coming to grips with fear.

Chapter 2

At that time a decree came down from the emperor Augustus, instructing everyone in the Roman world to register. This was the first census to be made during the rule of Quirinius, the governor of Syria, and everyone went to his own town to sign in.

Joseph went from Nazareth in Galilee to Judea, to Bethlehem, the city of David, his ancestor. He went there with Mary, his betrothed, who was pregnant, and they were there when it was time to deliver the baby. She gave birth to her first child, a son, and bundled him in cloth bands and placed him in a feeding trough. The hotel[1] didn't have enough room for them.[2]

Shepherds, country people, lived out in nearby fields guarding their sheep at night. An angel of the Lord stood in front of them and the splendor of the Lord illuminated the surroundings. They were terribly frightened.

But the angel said to them, "Don't be afraid.[3] I bring you a wonderful, joyful message intended for all people. Today in the city of David was born someone who will deliver you. He is anointed with oil, Christos, a master from the house of David.

"Here is what you should look for: a baby wrapped in bands of fabric and lying in a feeding trough."

Suddenly with the angel there appeared a huge army of sky beings praising God:

Glory to God high above
And here on earth
Peace to people
He blesses.

4   "Every person has his Bethlehem where new possibilities and hopes are born,
    where his history is invaded by novelty and the potency for new action.
    At such times the tyranny of the past and the terror of the future give way
    before a new time of open possibility—the vibrant present."
    —Sam Keen, *To a Dancing God* (New York: Harper & Row, 1970), 31

5   The shepherds are the ordinary laborers who will become the main part
    of Jesus's following. They also prefigure the idea of Jesus as shepherd, that
    is, one who tends and protects. The Greek meaning of the word "therapy"
    is one who serves and cares for others. Therefore, a shepherd is a kind of
    therapist for sheep. Jesus compares his Father in the Sky to a shepherd who
    goes out of his way to care for his sheep.

6   In India, seeing a holy teacher, a statue of a god or a goddess, or a holy place
    is called *darshan*. This experience can enliven the spirituality of anyone in the
    world, and here Simeon speaks in the language of *darshan*. He has seen with
    his own eyes. We, too, may need several moments of *darshan* in our lives,
    when we see with our own eyes a holy person, place, or event, to invigorate
    our spirituality. People of India sometimes travel with severe discomfort and
    cost for their *darshan*, and so can we. It is not an easy or simple matter to be
    in the right place and time to behold with our own eyes the mysteries that
    can move us ahead on our spiritual path.

7   In one strong, touching scene after the other, the myth of Christos is build-
    ing. Here Simeon, an old man, gives his sanction to the child. The child is
    initiated into a serious, indeed heroic, life. Here, in the beginning, the child
    and the old man each have a noble place, each honoring the other. Later the
    conflict will arise and develop to the point of the crucifixion.

When the angels had gone off into the sky, the shepherds said to each other, "Let's go to Bethlehem now and see the phenomenon they described to us."[4] They hurried off and found Mary and Joseph with the child lying in the feeding trough. After absorbing it all, they talked publicly about the things they had been told about this child. Everyone who heard was amazed at the shepherds' stories. Meanwhile, Mary quietly meditated on it all and kept the stories like a treasure in her heart.

The shepherds went back, praising and honoring God for all they had heard and seen and been told.[5]

Then, when eight days had gone by, it was time to circumcise the baby. They called him Jesus, the name mentioned by the angel before he was even conceived. Then, according to Mosaic law, it was time for purification. They brought the baby to Jerusalem to present him formally to the Lord. The law of the Lord states: "Every first child who is male has to be dedicated to the Lord." They also offered sacrifices to fulfill the requirements of the Lord's law: a pair of doves or pigeons.

In Jerusalem there was a man named Simeon, who was honorable and pious and hoped for Israel's relief. He had a holy spirit in him that had assured him he would not die until he had seen the Christos, the Lord's anointed one. Inspired by a spirit, he went into the temple and found the parents of the baby Jesus waiting for him to fulfill the requirements of the law. Simeon held the child and gave honor to God:

"Lord, you can let your servant go in peace now. I have seen with my own eyes[6] how, as promised, you offer us a way to freedom, how you are a light to inspire Gentiles and a beacon for your people, Israel."[7]

The child's mother and father were deeply moved to hear the things said about him.

8 With Anna, eighty-four years old, the initiation of the child Christos is
complete. The old man and the old woman acknowledge this young child's
future and his role in leading his people to a level of fulfillment never imagined even by the prophets.

Simeon blessed them and told Mary, the little one's mother, "This child will be inspired and will cause the rise and fall of many in Israel. He will be a controversial phenomenon. A sword will pass through your soul and he will reveal what weighs on many hearts."

There was a woman prophet there, too, Anna, the daughter of Phanuel, of the tribe Asher, and she was on in years. She had lived with her husband for seven years after they were married and as a widow until she was eighty-four. She never left the temple, worshipping night and day, fasting and praying. She approached the family and thanked God. Anyone hoping for the restoration of Jerusalem she told about the baby.[8]

When Joseph and Mary had done everything the law required of them, they returned to Galilee and their town of Nazareth. The child grew up strong and wise and enjoyed God's favor.

9 "To use the categories of Islamic thought, there is currently interest in *al-'amal* or action without *al-'ilm* or knowledge, whereas traditional Islamic sources have always taught that *al-'ilm* and *al-'amal* must accompany each other."
    —Seyyed Hossein Nasr, *Religion & the Order of Nature* (New York: Oxford University Press, 1996), 5

10 Jesus's response may seem cold and unnecessarily harsh, but he is merely stating the conditions of his life. He is called to a hero's destiny and that always requires a separation from one's parents. Notice the three days of being lost. The number three is prominent in fairy tales, and here it might hint that the account of Jesus's disappearance is indeed a story with deep significance. The three days here may foreshadow the three days between Jesus's death and resurrection. Perhaps there is a little forewarning here.

Once a year the parents went to Jerusalem for Passover, and the year he was twelve they went there as usual for the festival. When the celebration was over, they began to head back, but Jesus remained behind in Jerusalem, though his parents were unaware of it. They figured that he was with other pilgrims and so they traveled for a whole day before they began looking for him among their relatives and friends. But they didn't find him, so they went back to Jerusalem and looked all over for him.

Three days later they found him in the temple, sitting with the teachers, listening to them and raising questions. Everyone who heard him was astonished at his knowledge and his responses.[9]

When his parents saw him, they were surprised. His mother said, "Child, why have you done this to us? Your father and I have been worried sick looking all over for you."

"Why were you looking for me?" he said. "Don't you realize that I have to be in my father's house?"[10]

They didn't understand what he was saying, but he went back to Nazareth with them anyway and did what they asked of him.

His mother kept all these things in her heart, while Jesus grew up, acquiring wisdom and enjoying both human and divine favor.

1 "Recovery of the Tao is impossible without a complete transformation, a change of heart, which Christianity would call *metanoia*. Zen, of course, envisaged this problem, and studied how to arrive at *satori*, or the explosive rediscovery of the hidden and lost reality within us."
   —Thomas Merton, *Mystics and Zen Masters* (New York: Farrar, Straus and Giroux, 1967), 50

2 In preparation for our own work of forging a spiritual existence, a way that is both transcendent and sublime, we may have to work at smoothing and straightening the path. We need few diversions and detours and a way that is suited to us, comfortable, and direct. You do not instantly find your way to spiritual fulfillment.

3 Isaiah 40:3–5.

Chapter 3

It was the fifteenth year of the reign of Emperor Tiberius. Pontius Pilate was the governor of Judea and Herod ruled Galilee. His brother Philip was tetrarch of Iturea and Traconitis and Lysanias tetrarch of Abilene. Annas and Caiaphas were high priests. God's voice came to the son of Zechariah, John, when he was in the desert. He went out into the countryside in the area of the Jordan River introducing a baptism of *metanoia*, a fundamental shift in understanding that would relieve any guilt over serious transgression.[1]

This had been foretold in the words of the prophet Isaiah:

> *The sound of someone*
> *Shouting in the desert,*
> *"Clear a path for the Lord and*
> *Build a direct road for him.*[2]
> *Fill the gap in every valley*
> *And level every mountain and hill.*
> *Straighten out twisting roads*
> *And make bumpy lanes smooth.*
> *Every human being will see*
> *How God offers protection."*[3]

To the masses of people coming out for baptism, John said, "You sons and daughters of snakes. Who warned you to escape the upcoming catastrophe? You should be doing things that show that your hearts have changed.

"Don't tell each other, 'Abraham is our forefather.' I assure you that God can make children out of stones for Abraham. Even as we speak, the ax lies on the root of the trees. Any tree that doesn't bear good fruit will be cut down and tossed into the fire."

4   If you want to be part of the kingdom, included in a way of life that is in tune
     with the laws of existence and therefore profoundly fulfilling, you must stop
     thinking only of yourself and start giving of yourself to others. That is the
     secret of deep happiness: You are aligned with the law of life, which is a law
     of love.

5   The message of the Gospels has often been made more complicated than
     it needs to be. Here the idea is simple: Do your job without any hint of
     corruption.

6   *Christos* means "anointed" or a man for whom oil is the primary metaphor and
     epithet—raised to a high level of awareness and behavior.

7   We know this detail from Matthew 14.

8   With all his activities and teaching, you might overlook how often Jesus
     prays and meditates, as in this case. A connection to the Sky Father goes
     hand in hand with fashioning the utopian lifestyle.

9   Here is a strong indication that the sky is the location of spirit in the Gos-
     pels. Baptism means that you are prepared to shape a life suitable for the
     kingdom. Therefore, it will be a meaningful life. It is possible to waste and
     lose your life in distraction, unconsciousness, and acting out. Jesus goes
     through the rite of baptism and then the sky opens up. A voice praises him.
     This is what we all aspire to: a real, effective baptism, setting us off on a life
     that matters, and the sense that we are affirmed by the Sky Father, by the
     very heart and utterance of the source of life.

The people asked him, "Then what should we do?"[4]

He replied, "If you have two coats, give one to someone who doesn't have any. The same with someone who doesn't have any food."

Tax collectors arrived to be baptized and asked him, "Teacher, what should we do?"

"Collect only the amount as determined."

Then soldiers said, "What should we do?"

"Don't take money illegally with threats and accusations. Be satisfied with what you make honestly."[5]

The people were hopeful and expectant, wondering if John might be the Man of Oil.[6]

John answered them in this way: "I baptize you with water, but someone more significant is coming. I'm not good enough to even loosen his sandals. He will baptize you with a holy spirit and with fire."

He taught them many other things and announced the Great Teaching to the people.

Now, John had chastised Herod because of the affair of his brother's wife, Herodias,[7] and because of all the horrible things he had done. Meanwhile, Herod piled up more evil deeds by putting John in prison.

All the people present were baptized and Jesus, after his own baptism, was at prayer,[8] when suddenly the sky opened up and the holy spirit came down in the shape of a dove and a voice sounded from the sky, "You are my beloved son. You are a great joy to me."[9]

10 Jesus is both a man of earth and a son of the sky. Here his earthly father, Joseph, has a place of honor on the list of Jesus's ancestors.

When he started out, Jesus was around thirty. This is his lineage:

Joseph[10]
Heli
Matthat
Levi
Melchi
Jannai
Joseph
Mattathias
Amos
Nahum
Esli
Naggai
Maath
Mattahias
Semein
Josech
Joda
Joanan
Rhesa
Zerubbabel
Shealtiel
Neri
Melchi
Addi
Cosam
Elmadam
Er
Joshua
Eliezer
Jorim
Matthat
Levi

11 An acknowledgment of Jesus's Jewish ancestry.

Simeon
Judah
Joseph
Jonam
Eliakim
Melea
Menna
Mattatha
Nathan
David
Jesse
Obed
Boaz
Sala
Nahshon
Amminadab
Admin
Arni
Hezron
Perez
Judah
Jacob
Isaac
Abraham[11]
Terah
Nahor
Serug
Reu
Peleg
Eber
Shelah
Cainan
Arphaxad
Shem

12 We are all sons of Adam, of course, and so is Jesus. He is not just a spiritual
being but also a human one. When the Gospels refer to him as the "son of
man," maybe that epithet could be traced back to this reminder of his human
nature.

13 "The important thing for Luke was not alone to show that the God who lived
in Abraham was present in Jesus, but that the ancestry, the line of descent,
can be traced back still further, even to Adam and that Adam was a son of
the very Godhead, which means that he belonged to the time when humanity had just made the transition from a spiritual to a physical state."
    —Rudolf Steiner, *The Gospel of St. John* (n.p.: Anthroposophic Press, rev. ed.
        1962), 182

Noah
Lamech
Methuselah
Enoch
Jared
Mahalaleel
Cainan
Enos
Seth
Adam[12]
God[13]

1   Sometimes it is not easy to make the right choice when you are tempted to take a well-paying job that is somehow aligned with the "devil." This temptation is real and one that each of us may well face in the course of our lives.

2   Psalm 91:11–12.

3   These temptations resemble those of the Buddha, before his public life, and certainly our own. As we are deciding whether to live a life of service, compassion, and healing, we may be tempted by money, prestige, power, or security. You cannot serve any of these values exclusively and still be part of the Jesus kingdom.

Chapter 4

Fortified with a holy spirit, Jesus returned from the Jordan, and the spirit led him around in the desert, where the devil tested him for forty days. During that time he ate nothing, and when it was over he was very hungry. The devil told him, "If you're a son of God, tell this rock to become a loaf of bread."

Jesus responded, "It's been written, 'You don't live on just bread.'"

Then the devil brought him up to a high place to see all the countries in the world at once. He said to him, "I'll give you all this power and splendor. It's been given to me, and I can give it to anyone I want. If you just worship me, it's all yours."[1]

Jesus answered, "It's written, 'Worship the Lord your God and him only.'"

Then the devil whisked him off to Jerusalem and put him down on the highest point of the temple and said, "If you're a son of God, jump. It was written,

> 'He'll instruct his angels
> to protect you.
> They'll hold you up
> with their hands
> So that you don't smash your foot
> on a stone.'"[2]

Jesus told him, "Don't put the Lord your God to a test."[3]

When the devil had finished all his trials, he went away until another time.

4   Isaiah 61:1–2.

5   This saying about a prophet not being welcome in his hometown has special meaning in Jesus's case. He frequently warns that people will be complacent, feeling that they are in a special place of honor. The people in Jesus's hometown surely have a place in the kingdom. But they become especially upset when they hear Jesus's real message. It is not what they want, so they reject him.

6   A constant theme for the kingdom: Pay special attention to those not in your circle.

Restored by the spirit, Jesus returned to Galilee, where news about him spread throughout the region. He taught in synagogues and everyone spoke highly of him. Then he arrived at Nazareth, where he had grown up, and, as was his habit, he went to the synagogue on the Sabbath and stood to read. He opened the book of Isaiah and began:

> *"A spirit of the Lord is in me*
> *because he anointed me*
> *to bring the Great Teaching to the poor.*
> *He sent me to announce that prisoners will be set free,*
> *the blind will see, and the oppressed will have relief.*
> *I proclaim a year of the Lord's kindness."*[4]

He rolled up the scroll, handed it to the attendant, and sat down. The eyes of everyone present focused on him. Then he spoke:

"Today what you have heard—this scripture—is being fulfilled."

Everyone spoke highly of him and were surprised at the beautiful words that came out of his mouth. "Isn't this Joseph's son?" they asked.

He responded, "I know, you'll cite this old saying, 'Physician, heal yourself.' And you'll say, 'Do in your hometown what we've heard you did in Capernaum.' But I have to say to you in all earnestness, no prophet is welcome in his hometown.[5]

"I can tell you with certainty that in the days of Elijah, when there was no rain for three and a half years and a huge famine swept over the land, there were many widows in Israel. Still, Elijah was sent to none of them except Zarephath, a widow in the area of Sidon. At the time of the prophet Elisha there were many lepers in Israel. Except for Naaman the Syrian, none of them found relief."[6]

7   Often the Gospels speak of an "unclean spirit" and sometimes of a daimon (pl. daimons), and rarely of a devil. A daimon is not the same as a demon. For the Greeks it was a spirit, often unnamed, that either urged an action from within or warned against an action. Sometimes it had the role of a guardian angel. One of the most famous is Socrates's love daimon that, he says, guided his life. Sometimes I translate it as "daimonic" or "demonic force," stressing its inner quality and also subtly suggesting that it is a major factor for us to deal with today.

8   Today we are plagued by the daimonic as much as ever: fanaticism, narcissism, deep anger, prejudice, jealousy, greed. We do not see them as daimonic forces threatening the peace, and we do not know how to deal with them. Jesus, on the other hand, understands the daimonic and has power over it, encouraging us to find our own ways to deal with it effectively.

9   You might think of Jesus here as a shaman, one who travels in realms of the spiritual imagination. The daimons are of that domain, too, and recognize that he is familiar with their world.

When they heard all this, all the people in the synagogue were furious. They stood up and forced him out of the town and brought him to the hilltop on which they had built their town, intending to throw him over the edge. But he walked past them and went on his way.

Then he went on to Capernaum, a town in Galilee, and taught on the Sabbath. The people were astonished at his teachings, especially at the authority in his message.

There happened to be a man in the synagogue who was possessed by the spirit of an unclean daimon.[7] He screamed out loudly, "Jesus of Nazareth, leave us be. What could we possibly have to do with each other? Have you come to annihilate us? I recognize you. You're God's holy one."

Jesus spoke out sharply, "Quiet! Come out of him!" Then the daimon hurled the man down in front of the people and came out of him without having done any harm. The people were in shock. They said to one another, "What does this mean? He gives orders to unclean daimons with authority and power, and they come out." Word about him spread to every place in the region.[8]

Then he rose and left the synagogue and went into Simon's house. Simon's mother-in-law happened to be suffering from a fever and they asked him about her. Jesus stood over her and admonished the fever and it left her. She got up right away and tended them.

The sun was going down and many brought their sick, people with all kinds of problems, to him, and he laid his hand on each one, caring for them. Daimons were coming out of many people, shrieking, "You are the son of God." But he chastised them and wouldn't let them speak. They knew that he was Christos.[9]

10 The word used here, a form of *euangelon*, or evangel, is usually translated as "good news" or "good tidings." In context, it is a key term that refers to the message or teaching about the kingdom. Sometimes I refer to it as the "Great Teaching."

At daylight Jesus went out to a remote place, and the people looked all over for him. They approached him and wanted to keep him from continuing his journey. But he told them, "I have to spread the word about the Great Teaching[10] and the kingdom of God to other towns, too. This is why I was sent." So he went on speaking in the synagogues of Judea.

1 Carl Jung points out that the astrological era of Pisces, the sign of the fish, comes last in the zodiac, thus preparing for profound renewal. See C. G. Jung, *Aion: Researches into the Phenomenology of the Self*, edited by Gerhard Adler and R. F. C. Hull, in *Collected Works of C. J. Jung*, vol. 9, part 2 (Princeton, NJ: Princeton University Press, 1968), sec. 174. This fits in with our main theme of Jesus inaugurating a utopian vision for humanity. His followers are fishermen, gathering people as though they were fish into the "net" of the kingdom.

2 The point is to "catch" all of humanity in the net of the Jesus way and thus raise it to a new level of understanding, where love rules.

3 Apparently, there is a subtle reversal here as well. Casting nets was an image often used in a negative way, referring to temptations that might snare people, as in a net. Here, in Jesus's terms, the students become fishermen of people, catching them and drawing them into the kingdom. See Robert H. Eisenman, *James the Brother of Jesus: The Key to Unlocking the Secrets of Early Christianity and the Dead Sea Scrolls* (New York: Penguin Books, 1997), 712–715.

Chapter 5

On one occasion Jesus was standing by the lake of Gennesaret and a crowd was pressing around him to hear the word of God. He noticed two boats anchored at the edge of the lake. The fishermen had climbed out of them and were washing their nets.[1] He got into one of the boats, Simon's, and asked him to put out a little from the shore. He sat down and taught the people from the boat.

When he had finished speaking, he said to Simon, "Put out into the deep water and drop your nets for a catch. Simon answered, "Master, we labored all night and caught nothing, but I'll do what you say and put the nets out."

When they did this, they amassed such a great number of fish that their nets started to tear. They signaled their coworkers in the other boat to come and help them. They joined them and filled both boats to the point of nearly sinking. When Simon Peter saw all this, he bent down to Jesus's feet and said, "Keep a distance from me, Lord, for I am an imperfect person." He and his fellow workers were stunned at the number of fish they had netted.[2]

James and John, sons of Zebedee and Simon's partners, were also amazed. Jesus said to Simon, "Don't worry, from now on you'll be catching people." They pulled their boats up onto the shore and left everything behind and joined up with him.[3]

Jesus was in one of the cities when a man covered in leprosy saw him and fell down on his face and begged him, "Lord, if it is your pleasure, you can clear up my body."

4 It is extraordinary for Jesus to have touched an outcast.

5 The Greek word here, *catharisai*, is a form of "catharsis," one of the chief technical terms for healing in the Gospels. Aristotle uses the word to describe the clarifying that takes place in theater, and psychoanalysis uses it to describe the clearing out that psychotherapy can accomplish. Having been afflicted with family and cultural blockages and having made mistakes ourselves, we all need catharsis.

6 Here we see teaching, healing, and prayer in one paragraph that offers a good model for how to be in the kingdom.

7 The word for "heal" here is *iasthai*, which is related to the name of a Greek goddess of healing, Iaso, often pictured with Panacea. Allusions to several Greek gods and goddesses underlie the Gospel text. Another related word is *iatros*, meaning a physician. So the word used here really means "to cure." A more common word in the Gospels often translated as "heal" is *therapeia*. It means to nurse, serve, or take care of.

8 This is usually translated as "sins." I want to avoid many of the moralistic connotations of that word without losing the sense of deep ignorance and mistake that the Greek word *hamartia* implies. Historian Karen L. King's comments are helpful in this regard: "To sin means that people turn away from God toward concern for the material world and the body because they have been led astray by the passions."
   —King, *The Gospel of Mary of Magdala: Jesus and the First Woman Apostle* (Santa Rosa, CA: Polebridge Press, 2013), 50

Or *hamartia* may be, as Aristotle says, a misguided deed done out of severe ignorance. Many people today seem to lack a deeply felt idea of justice, community, and personal excellence. They are ignorant about basic human qualities.

Jesus extended his hand, touched him,[4] and said, "It is my pleasure. Clear up!"[5] Instantly the leprosy left him. Jesus instructed him to say nothing. "But go and show yourself to the priest and make an offering for your cleansing, as Moses required, as a testimony."

Word about Jesus was spreading farther and great crowds came together to listen to him and have their suffering eased. Jesus would often go off to the wilderness to pray.[6]

One day, as he was teaching, some Pharisees and lawyers were sitting nearby. They had traveled from every town in Galilee and Judea, and some from Jerusalem. He had power from the Lord to heal.[7] Some men were carrying a man on a bed. He was paralyzed, and they were attempting to bring him in and put him down in front of Jesus. They couldn't find a way to get him inside, the crowd was so big, so they went up on the roof and let him down on his cot through the roofing and into the thick of the crowd and in front of Jesus.

Seeing the depth of their trust, he said, "Dear man, you are relieved of the burden of your faults."[8]

The experts in the law and the Pharisees discussed this. "Who is this who utters blasphemy? Who but God can offer relief from guilt?"

Jesus was aware of their conversation and said, "Why are your hearts full of these thoughts? Is it easier to say, 'You are relieved of your guilt' or 'Stand up and walk'? So you understand that the son of man has the authority here on earth to relieve people of guilt," he told the paralyzed man, "I ask you to stand up, pick up your cot, and go home." He got up right away, picked up the cot he had been lying on, and went home, giving honor to God. Everyone was shocked and praised God. Actually, they were terrified and said, "We have seen some astonishing things today."

9   Note that Jesus is once more at dinner among people with whom you would not expect him to associate. They are sharing a meal, an important image in all the Gospels. Whom do you eat with? That question is important and revealing. Jesus eats not only with his loyal followers, but also with those outside his circle. The Gospels keep trying to impress this point: Do not just be with people like you. Teach, heal, and be a good example for those different from you in lifestyle, background, and values.

10 The Gospels propose a new way of life, radical and utopian, based on mutual regard (*agape*), healing, forgiveness, and friendship. The old way is self-centered, narcissistic, and rule-bound. The new way is radically different; you cannot keep the old way and tweak it to resemble the new one.

Then Jesus went out and caught sight of a tax collector named Levi sitting in the revenue booth. He said, "Follow me." Levi left everything behind and got up and joined Jesus. Then Levi gave a big dinner for him in his house, where a large group of people, including revenue officers and others, sat around the table.⁹

The Pharisees and experts in the law complained to his followers, "Why do you eat and drink with revenue clerks and other riffraff?

Jesus replied, "The healthy don't need a doctor; the sick do. I'm not here to invite innocent people to *metanoia*, or change of heart, but those who have done wrong."

In answer they said, "John's followers frequently pray and fast and the Pharisees' followers do the same thing. But your followers eat and drink."

Jesus said, "You really can't ask the friends of the groom to go without eating while the groom is with them, can you? Eventually the groom will be taken away. Then they can fast."

Then he spoke in parables: "You wouldn't tear a piece of cloth from a new coat and put it on an old one. If you did, you'd rip the new one, and the swatch from the new one wouldn't match the old one.

"You wouldn't put new wine into old winebags; if you did, the new wine would break the skins and pour out, and you'd ruin the winebags. You should put new wine into new winebags. After drinking a vintage wine, no one wants a new wine. You say, 'The old is fine.'"¹⁰

1   The word "some" is important here. Not all Pharisees were rigid legalists, a conclusion that many reach after a surface reading of the Gospels. You see moralistic anxiety everywhere: education, medicine, politics, law enforcement, and, of course, religion.

2   Another plank in the kingdom philosophy: Human concerns are more important than religious rules. It is difficult for many spiritual people to grasp this teaching, perhaps because they were brought up to think of religion as maintaining virtue, and virtue was defined as following the rules. The Jesus approach is not as liberating as it may look. To transcend rules and serve humanity in the end is much more demanding.

3   If you are governed by burdensome rules, especially if they are self-imposed, you do not like to see others living freely and at ease. Deep inside, you want them to suffer under the rules, too. Your displeasure may turn to anger, and anger to violence.

Chapter 6

Once, when Jesus was strolling through fields of wheat on a Sabbath, his followers picked at the heads, crushed them in their hands, and ate the wheat. Some[1] Pharisees said, "Why do you break the law of the Sabbath?"

Jesus answered them, "Have you ever read what David did when he and his companions were hungry? He went into the house of God and ate holy bread and gave it to his friends, which is certainly not legal. Only priests can eat that bread. The son of man is Lord of the Sabbath."[2]

On another Sabbath he went to the synagogue to teach, when a man with a withered hand appeared. The Pharisees and experts in the law observed closely to see if he would heal on the Sabbath. Then they could criticize him.

He knew what they were thinking and said to the man with the bad hand, "Stand up and come over here."

The man stood and came forward.

Jesus said to him, "Let me ask you a question. Is it legal to do good or harm on the Sabbath, to save a life or kill it?"

He gazed at all of them and said to the man, "Hold out your hand." When he did so, the hand was like new.

The others were furious and considered what they could do to Jesus.[3]

4 Here, in the midst of breaking the rules and feeding people and dining with questionable associates, Jesus spends a night praying on a mountain with his closest students. The kingdom is both earthly and spiritual, both Epicurean and mildly ascetic. The mountain suggests a movement upward and away from earthly concerns. But note that Jesus is usually in the valleys—healing on the streets, dining in homes, teaching from a boat. He is among the people and fully immersed in life.

5 The word is a form of *ouranos*, the sky, and therefore suggests an "ouranic" reward—of the sky, or spiritual. We have our earth pleasures and our sky pleasures.

One day he withdrew to a mountain to pray and spent the entire night praying to God.⁴ At daylight he called his followers and selected twelve of them to be his representatives, apostles: Simon, whom he called Peter; Andrew, Simon's brother; James; John; Philip; Bartholomew; Matthew; Thomas; James, the son of Alophaeus; Simon, known as the Zealot; Judas, the son of James; and Judas Iscariot, who was to be a traitor.

Jesus came down from the mountain and stood on level ground, where a huge crowd of followers and people from Judea, Jerusalem, and the coastal areas of Tyre and Sidon had gathered. They had come to hear him and have their illnesses treated. He also tended to people with unclean spirits. Everyone made an effort to touch him because there was a power emanating from him, healing everything.

He turned and looked at his followers and said,

"Fortunate are you who are poor. The kingdom of God is yours.

"Fortunate are you who are now hungry. You'll feel fed.

"Fortunate are you who are sad and weepy now. You'll be laughing.

"Fortunate are you whom people despise because of the son of man, and reject you and say bad things about you and think that what you are called is wicked. Be happy and dance for joy. Your spiritual⁵ reward will be great. Remember that their fathers used to treat the prophets in the same way.

"Watch out if you're wealthy. You're enjoying your comforts now.

"Watch out if you have plenty to eat now. You'll be hungry.

"Watch out if you laugh now. You'll be sad and cry.

"Watch out if people speak well of you now. Their ancestors used to treat the false prophets in the same way.

"This is what I say: 'Love your enemies. Be good to those who hate you. Bless those who curse you. Pray for those who treat you badly.'

6 "The turning of the other cheek is not a thing that any social collectivity could put into practice with a view to maintaining its equilibrium, and it has no meaning except as a spiritual attitude; the spiritual man alone firmly takes his stand outside the logical chain of individual reactions, since for him a participation in the current of these reactions is tantamount to a fall from grace."
      —James S. Cutsinger, ed., *The Fullness of God: Frithjof Schuon on Christianity* (Bloomington, IN: World Wisdom, 2004), 11

7 This whole passage is riddled with the word *agape*, a special neighborly love and deep respect. It also presents a radical statement of values for the kingdom that go against natural and unconscious ways of relating. It is a challenge to "default" reality.

8 *Agape* is an opening of the heart and often includes the feeling of empathy. "Where Paul uses the word *love*, Jesus uses the word *compassion*. The associations of the word in Aramaic and Hebrew are strikingly evocative: to be compassionate is to be 'womblike': life-giving, nourishing, embracing. So God is; so we are to be."
      —Marcus J. Borg, *The Heart of Christianity: Rediscovering a Life of Faith* (San Francisco: HarperSanFrancisco, 2003), 122

"If someone hits you in the face, turn the other cheek.[6] If someone steals your coat, give him your shirt, too. Give to anyone at all who asks something of you, and if someone takes what is yours, don't ask for it back. Treat others the way you would like them to treat you. If you love those who love you, what good is that? The wicked love those who love them.[7]

"If you are good to those who are good to you, what does that make you? Immature people do that. If you lend things to people you expect to give you something in return, where is the merit in that? Even self-serving people lend to their own kind to get back exactly as much as they offered.

"Love your enemies, do good, and offer something without expecting anything in return. Then your reward will be abundant and you'll be children of God. He is good even to insensitive and dishonest people. Have empathy, just as your Father has empathy.[8] Don't criticize, and you won't be criticized. Don't condemn, and you won't be condemned. Let people be, and you will be free to be. Give, and you will have things given to you. Indeed, things will pour into your lap as if they were gathered together, mixed up, and overflowing. How much you give is how much you will get in return."

He gave them a parable: "A blind man can't guide a blind man or they will both fall into a hole. A follower isn't above his teacher, and yet, when he has been educated, he'll be just like his teacher.

"Why do you notice the tiny particle in your brother's eye but fail to see the tree trunk in your own? How can you say to him, 'Brother, let me remove that tiny particle from your eye,' when you don't see the tree trunk in your own? You're a hypocrite. Remove the tree trunk from your own eye first and then the tiny particle in your brother's eye.

9 One of Jesus's main concerns is fostering an inner base for spiritual behavior. It is not enough to follow the rules or perform the outer traditional rituals. You must cultivate inner qualities that lead to corresponding actions.

"A fine tree never bears bad fruit, and a bad tree never bears good fruit. Every tree can be spotted by its own kind of fruit. You don't gather figs from thorn bushes or grapes from thistles. A good person brings good things from the positive treasury of his heart. The bad person brings evil out of the evil storehouse of his heart. A person's mouth speaks from what is overflowing in his heart.[9]

"Why do you call me 'Master' and don't do what I say?

"I'll describe to you what kind of person comes to me, listens to what I have to say, and acts accordingly. He is like a person building a house. He digs deep and puts the foundation on solid rock. If a flood were to come, the floodwaters would smash against the house but wouldn't even shake it because it was so well built.

"But a person who has heard and doesn't act accordingly is like a person who sets his house on the earth without a foundation. The floodwaters would smash against it and cause it to collapse. The house would be a disaster."

1   An occupying soldier says that he is not worthy to have Jesus in his house.
    He is an unlikely person to be a citizen of Jesus's kingdom, and yet he is
    there explicitly. Jesus recognizes his special capacity to trust and to show
    real humility, qualities of those embracing the new kingdom.

2   "Christians along with other men are called on to build the boundaryless
    community, the body of man identified with the body of Christos, though
    all men are free to symbolize it in their own way."
        —Robert N. Bellah, *Beyond Belief: Essays on Religion in a Post-Traditionalist World*
        (Berkeley: University of California Press, 1991), 228

Chapter 7

When Jesus finished speaking to an attentive crowd, he went to Capernaum. He met a centurion there whose highly respected servant was sick and on the edge of death. The centurion had heard of Jesus and had sent some elders from among the Jews to him, asking him to come and help the servant. When they spoke to Jesus, they begged him, "This person is worth your attention. He loves our country and built our synagogue."

Jesus went off with them and was not far from the house when the centurion sent friends to tell him, "Sir, don't bother. I am not worthy that you come under my roof.[1] This is why I didn't feel right in coming to you. Just say a word and my servant will be cured. I'm someone who works under authority and have soldiers under me. If I tell one of them, 'Go,' he goes. If I say to another one, 'Come,' he comes. If I tell my servant, 'Do this,' he does it."

When Jesus heard all this, he was impressed. He turned to the crowd following him and said, "I have to say, I haven't found such trust in Israel."[2]

When the delegation returned to the house, they found the servant in good health.

3 The stories in Luke's Gospel always speak on many levels at once. You may read this story, if you wish, as a literal, historical account of Jesus raising someone from death. Or you may read it as a metaphor. Just as the blind see, which could mean that people who have not formerly been able to see what life is about suddenly develop a new kind of vision, so those who are soul-dead, unconscious and unaware, develop the ability to better see life for what it is.

Some time later Jesus went to a town called Nain. His followers were with him, and a huge crowd followed them. As he approached the city gate, people were carrying a dead person out, his mother's only son, and she was a widow. A group of people from the town accompanied her.

When the master saw her, he was deeply upset and said, "Don't cry."

He went and touched the coffin, and the pallbearers stopped. He said, "Young man, I tell you, wake up." The dead man sat up and spoke. Jesus gave him to his mother.[3]

They were all terrified and praised God, "A great prophet has appeared among us. God has looked kindly on his people."

Word about Jesus spread all over Judea and the surrounding region.

John's disciples told him about all these events, and he asked two of them to go to the master and say, "Are you the one we've been expecting or should we wait for someone else?"

In that time Jesus had helped many people with their illnesses and afflictions and evil spirits and had restored sight to many blind people. So he answered, "Go and tell John what you've heard and seen: The blind see, the lame walk, lepers are clean, the deaf hear, those who are not alive wake up, and the poor receive the Great Teaching. Anyone not scandalized by me is in bliss."

When John's representatives had gone, Jesus spoke to the people about John. "What did you go into the wilderness to see? A reed shaken by the wind? What did you go out to see? A man dressed in comfortable clothes? Those who are smartly dressed live in luxury in palaces. What did you go out to see? A prophet? Yes, and I say, more than a prophet.

"This is someone about whom it was written, 'Look, I'm sending my representative ahead of you. He will prepare a path for you.'

4   You can be famous and revered in the eyes of others, but if you are not living the kingdom values you are lower than anyone in the kingdom. It is more important to live with compassion and humanity than to be praised by your peers.

5   The kingdom is a state of mind in which you trust yourself and discover the rules of life. But people usually put their faith in authority figures, who become angry if people do not do what they are told. One of the scandals in Jesus's presence is his habit of assuming his own authority. But this is not egotistical, because he refers everything to his Father in the Sky.

6   Notice that this woman is not named. She is "the woman with the alabaster jar." She is not Mary of Magdala. I call her a "lost soul" instead of a sinner, to keep the moralism out of the language. This scene is important on many levels: Jesus is recognized as the Man of Oil and Jesus the Epicurean; it offers the confounding idea that to enter this idealistic, utopian kingdom it actually helps that you are coming from a place of misguided behavior and serious mistakes. Your past life of indulgence and misbehavior makes you human, a good place to be when you consider becoming idealistic.

"I'm saying to you that of those born of a woman no one is greater than John. At the same time, anyone lowest in the kingdom of God is greater than he is."4

When the crowd and the revenue clerks heard this, they respected God's plan, for they had been through John's baptism. But the Pharisees and the legal figures rejected God's plan for them. They hadn't received John's baptism.

And Jesus said, "What are the people of this generation like? What can I compare them to? They're like children sitting and shouting to each other in the marketplace.

> " 'We played the flute for you,
> and you didn't dance.
> We sang a lament,
> and you didn't cry.'5

"John the Baptist came and didn't eat bread or drink wine and you said he had a devil in him. The son of man comes and he eats and drinks and you say, 'Look, a glutton and a drunk, a friend of revenue officers and derelicts.'

"But all her children give witness to wisdom."

One of the Pharisees asked him to have dinner with him, and so he went into the Pharisee's house and sat at the table. There was a woman in town who had a bad reputation. When she discovered that Jesus was sitting at the table in a Pharisee's house, she brought an alabaster jar full of perfume. She placed herself behind him at his feet and cried and wet his feet with her tears, wiping them with her hair, and she kissed his feet and rubbed them with fragrant oil.

The Pharisee who was Jesus's host saw all this and thought to himself, "If this man were indeed a prophet, he would know what kind of woman this is touching him, truly a lost soul."6

Jesus said, "Simon, I want to tell you something."

"Tell me."

7   "In a manner not yet understood of the world he [Christ] regarded sin and
    suffering as being in themselves beautiful, holy things and modes of perfec-
    tion. It seems a very dangerous idea. It is—all great ideas are dangerous.
    That it was Christ's creed admits of no doubt. That it is the true creed I don't
    doubt myself."
         —Oscar Wilde, "De Profundis," in The Complete Works of Oscar Wilde (New York:
         Harper & Row, 1989), 933

8   This passage on forgiveness concludes with Jesus asserting once again the
    power of trust. As philosopher Paul Tillich explains, "The courage to be . . .
    is the courage to accept the forgiveness of sins . . . as the fundamental expe-
    rience in the encounter with God. Self-affirmation in spite of the anxiety of
    guilt and condemnation presupposes participation in something that tran-
    scends the self." See Tillich, The Courage to Be (New Haven, CT: Yale Univer-
    sity Press, 1952), 165. The woman with the alabaster jar trusts and thus is
    able to be forgiven. You cannot prove that the Jesus way will bless your life,
    but you can trust it, if you are convinced of its beauty and wisdom.

"A moneylender had two people in his debt. One owed him five hundred denarii and the other fifty. Neither could repay their loans, and he graciously forgave them both. Which one will love him more?"

Simon responded, "The one who owed more, I'm sure."

"That's right."[7]

Turning to the woman, Jesus said to Simon. "See this woman? I came into your house and you didn't offer me any water for my feet, and yet she has wet my feet with her tears and wiped them off with her hair. You didn't embrace me, but from the time I came in she hasn't stopped kissing my feet. You didn't give me any oil for my hair, but she rubbed my feet with fragrant perfume. This is why I say that her faults, which are certainly many, are pardoned, because she has so much love. Whoever has little to forgive doesn't love as much."

Then he told her, "You're released from your errant ways."

The people sitting at the table said to each other, "Who is this that he can forgive transgressions?"

To the woman he said, "Your trust has saved you.[8] You can leave in peace."

1 This passing observation about the women who are part of Jesus's circle and support him financially is significant. It tells us that Jesus is not only with a male crowd of friends and followers. It also echoes the teaching style of the Greek philosopher Epicurus, who has many values in common with Jesus—friendship, food, companionship, and simplicity. Epicurus also taught in a group of men and women friends.

2 "The purpose of the Sower parable, as many think, was, like that of most of the parables, eschatological: it had to do with the breaking-in of the kingdom of God, here represented by the harvest, a traditional figure for it. Between sowing and harvest many frustrations occur; but when the harvest comes, and the angel puts in his sickle, all will be fruition and triumph."
    —Frank Kermode, *The Genesis of Secrecy: On the Interpretation of Narrative* (Cambridge, MA: Harvard University Press, 1979), 32

Chapter 8

Afterward, Jesus went from town to town, giving people the welcome message about the kingdom of God. The twelve joined him, along with some women who had been helped with evil spirits and illnesses—Mary of Magdala, from whom seven daimons had come out; Joanna, the wife of Cuza, the steward in Herod's house; Susanna; and several others. These women used their own resources to offer support.[1]

As a crowd was assembling and people were coming to Jesus from many towns, he told this parable: "A farmer sowed some seed, and as he was sowing some fell on the road. People walked on it and birds came and ate it. Some fell on rocky ground, and when the plants appeared they dried up because they didn't have enough moisture. Some seeds fell among weeds that sprouted with them and choked them. But some seeds fell on good soil. These came up and yielded a crop that was a hundred times what was planted."

After telling the story he yelled out, "If you are not deaf, listen."

His followers asked him what the parable meant.

He said, "You are allowed to know the mysteries of the kingdom of God, but the others get the message in parables, so that even though they see, they don't really perceive, and though they hear, they don't understand.[2]

"Here is what the parable is about: The seed is the word of God. The ones near the road are those who have heard, but then the devil comes and takes the word out of their heart. They don't trust, and so they are not saved. The ones on rocky ground are those who hear and accept the word happily but have no deep roots. They believe for a while, but they fall away when they're tempted.

3 It is worth asking how and to what extent the gospel teaching has borne fruit over the centuries. Many have found a conscience and have made large and small contributions to humanity. But sometimes it seems that the teaching has not borne fruit except to give people a set of beliefs and a shorthand kind of moral philosophy—an authoritative list of dos and don'ts. The gospel idea of "fruit" is much more challenging and real.

4 In context, this would seem to mean that, if you have the makings of a visionary, community-minded, and fair person, you will derive more from Jesus's way as you become better acquainted with the Jesus philosophy. If you do not have the basics, you will not understand or appreciate what the utopian kingdom is all about.

5 "Every intellect must submit itself through faith to the Word of God and hear with utmost attention that *inward* teaching of the supreme Master."
—Nicolas of Cusa, "On the Vision of God," in *Nicolas of Cusa: Selected Spiritual Writings*, translated by H. Lawrence Bond, Classics of Western Spirituality (New York: Paulist Press, 1997), 286 [emphasis mine]

6 You must step beyond modern science, perhaps, to appreciate how powerful you can be if you adopt the values of the Jesus kingdom. You may discover a new beneficial kinship with nature.

"The seeds that fell among weeds are those who have heard, but as they go along they are suffocated with worldly preoccupations, wealth, and entertainments. Their fruit doesn't come to maturity.

"But the seeds on good soil are those who have heard the word with a sincere and well-meaning heart and persevere and bear fruit.[3]

"If you light a lamp, you don't cover it with a bowl or put it under a bed. You place it on a stand so that anyone coming in will have some light. Nothing that is hidden will fail to be revealed, and all secrets will be known and come to light.

"Listen to this carefully. Whoever has something will have more given to him. Whoever has nothing, even what he thinks he has will be taken away."[4]

His mother and brothers arrived and couldn't reach him because of all the people. Someone said, "Your mother and brothers are standing outside and want to see you."

He said, "My mother and brothers are those who hear the word of God and heed it."[5]

One day Jesus and his followers got into a boat, and he said to them, "Let's go to the other side of the lake." So they set out. As they were sailing, he fell asleep. A strong wind blew in on the lake and threatened to swamp them. They went to Jesus and woke him up. "Master, we're in trouble." He got up and ordered the wind and pounding waves to stop, and they calmed down.

He said to them, "Where is your trust?" They were terrified and amazed and said to one another, "Who is this? He commands the winds and the water and they obey him."[6]

7   "The destructive energies that cause mental instability and emotional anguish."
    —Elaine Pagels, *Beyond Belief: The Secret Gospel of Thomas* (New York: Random
    House, 2003), 7

The meaning ascribed to daimons should not be "devil" but "possession."
Everyone has some form of possession in life, from mild to extreme, as in
a serious bout of jealousy or depression. And for most of us the daimon is
indeed plural. Many powerful forces inspire us to do things we later regret.

8   People are both drawn to Jesus for his powers of healing and terrified by
    those same powers, especially when they involve possession. Clearly, Jesus
    had a powerful presence, so strong that it terrified people. We, too, can have
    that kind of power and presence if we get in tune with the laws of life, the
    Tao, the way things work. To this Jesus always adds the element of trust.

They sailed to the region of Gerasenes, across from Galilee. When Jesus got out of the boat and stood on land, a man from the town who was daimonically possessed came up to him. It had been a long time since he had worn clothes, and he lived among the tombs, rather than in a house.

He spotted Jesus and yelled out and fell down in front of him and in a loud voice said, "What do we have in common, Jesus, son of the God above? Please, don't torture me."

Jesus commanded the unclean spirit to come out of the man. It had held him captive many times, and he was tied up in chains and shackles and kept under surveillance. Still, he could break his irons and then feel driven into the desert by the daimon.

Jesus asked him, "What's your name?" He answered, "Legion"—many daimons[7] had gone into him. They were begging Jesus not to order them to come out and go into the abyss. A herd of pigs was grazing on the mountainside, and the daimons begged Jesus to let them go into the pigs, and he agreed. The daimons left the man and entered the pigs, and then the herd stampeded down the steep bank into the lake and drowned.

When the herdsmen saw what had taken place, they ran away and told everyone in town and in the countryside. Then, of course, people came out to see what was going on. They came to Jesus and found the man whose daimons had been expelled. He was sitting at Jesus's feet, properly clothed and clear-headed. But they were frightened.

Those who had seen the event described how the man was previously troubled by daimons and now was better. Then everyone from the Gerasenes area asked Jesus to leave. By now they were terrified.[8]

So Jesus got into the boat and went back. The man who had been possessed asked to go along, but Jesus sent him away. "Go home and bear witness to all that God has done for you." So he went off, telling everyone how much Jesus had done for him.

9 Ask a doctor, a nurse, a therapist, or a teacher what it is like to be in a healing mode all day long. It is draining in a particular way. You sense the power
   going out of you for the benefit of a patient, a client, or a student.

10 Jesus is always aware of the need for food, an example of his profound Epi-
   cureanism. The Greek philosopher Epicurus understood the deep need in
   human beings for food, not just for nourishment but for restoration in every
   respect.

On his return, Jesus found a welcoming crowd of people waiting for him. A leader from the synagogue, a man named Jairus, kneeled in front of Jesus and begged him to come to his house. His only daughter, now twelve years old, was dying.

As Jesus walked, the crowd surrounded him. Among them was a woman who had suffered from internal bleeding for twelve years. She had spent all her money on physicians, but none could help her. She came up behind him and touched the edge of his garment and instantly the bleeding stopped.

Jesus asked, "Who touched me?"

No one said anything, and so Peter said, "Master, the people are surrounding you and pushing up against you."

Jesus said, "Someone touched me. I sensed power going out of me."[9]

The woman realized that she couldn't keep her secret, so she approached him, trembling, and bowed down in front of him. She explained to everyone why she had touched him and that she had been helped instantly.

He told her, "Daughter, your trust has made you better. Go in peace."

While he was talking, someone from the leader's house came and said, "Your daughter is dead. Don't trouble the teacher any longer."

Jesus heard this and said, "Don't be afraid. Trust, and she will be safe."

When he arrived at the house, he didn't let anyone go in with him except Peter, John, and James, and the child's mother and father. They were all crying and sobbing. But Jesus said, "Don't cry. She isn't dead. She's sleeping."

They scoffed at this. They knew she was dead. But he took her hand and called out, "Child, wake up." Her spirit came back and she got up immediately. Jesus told them to give her something to eat.[10] Her parents were shocked, but he told them not to tell anyone what had happened.

1   Teaching and healing are the key activities of Jesus's followers when they go
     out on their mission, and they go with nothing, in a spirit of poverty, not
     owning or possessing anything. The purity and simplicity of this mission
     stands in contrast to wealthy churches and ministers today. We take this
     development lightly, but we could be more attuned to perceiving the spirit
     of Jesus's mission.

2   The twelve have a good, practical idea about feeding all the people, but
     Jesus rejects it. In the Gospel stories you always have to keep the subtext in
     mind. When Jesus heals a blind person, think about how we are all blind to
     what is happening in our lives. When he talks about feeding people, remem-
     ber that one of his missions is to feed people's souls, as he did at the Last
     Supper. In that way, this story of the bread and fish is like other stories that
     tell how to establish the kingdom with the smallest efforts.

Chapter 9

Jesus called the twelve together. He gave them power over all daimons and to care for the sick. Then he sent them out to heal the sick and to proclaim the kingdom of God. He told them, "Take nothing with you on your trip—no staff, no luggage, no bread, no money. Not even extra clothing. When you go into a house, stay there until you leave that city. If someone doesn't welcome you, when you leave that city, shake the dirt off your feet as a gesture."[1]

So they went out to the villages, giving people the welcome message and caring for them everywhere.

Herod, the tetrarch, heard all about what was going on and was deeply disturbed. Some said that John had risen from the dead and some that Elijah had appeared and others that one of the old prophets had resurrected.

Herod said, "I had John beheaded myself, so who is this man I'm hearing such things about?" He wanted badly to see him.

When the apostles returned, they told Jesus everything that had happened to them. He took them with him and went off alone to a city called Bethsaida. But the crowds caught on and followed him. He welcomed them and spoke to them about the kingdom of God and cared for those in need of healing.

Toward the end of the day the twelve came to him and said, "Send the people away so they can go to the nearby villages and countryside to find lodging and food. This is a remote area."

He said, "No, you give them something to eat."[2]

3   Again, the Ouranos archetype. Here is the Orphic hymn to Ouranos that
    suggests the degree of holiness attached to him (it) and correspondences
    with the Gospel Father:

> Ouranos,
> Father of Everything,
> Eternal substance of the Cosmos,
> Self-creating,
> Source of all, End of all,
> Father of the Universe,
> Spinning sphere-like around Earth,
> Home of the blessed gods,
> You move like a roaring whirlwind.
> You embrace everything,
> Protecting all things
> On earth and in the sky.
> In your heart lies nature's
> Insurmountable necessity.
> Deep-blue, impenetrable,
> Shimmering, polymorphous,
> All-seeing Father of Kronos,
> Holy and sublime daimon.
> Listen. Grant a holy way of life
> To those just initiated.
>   —Thomas Moore; previously unpublished translation

4   It might be distracting to focus on the magical and miraculous nature of this
    story of the bread and fish. Instead, you might think deeply about the need
    to nourish people, both physically and spiritually.

5   Of course, the history of anointing and the Messiah in Judaism is important
    background for this statement. But we can also consider that, apart from
    history, Christos signifies anyone who has found a way to shift in awareness
    and lifestyle through *metanoia* to an intensified way of life. "Christos" means
    "oiled," raised to a special level, living as a fully rounded human being of
    remarkable understanding and compassion.

They said, "All we have are five loaves of bread and two fish. Maybe we should go and buy food for everyone." There were nearly five thousand people. He said to the followers, "Tell them to sit down in groups of about fifty each."

They did so and everyone sat down. Then he took the five loaves of bread and the two fish and looked up to the sky.[3] He blessed them and broke them up and gave them to the followers to offer to the people. Everyone ate to their satisfaction, and the bits of food that were left over filled twelve baskets.[4]

Later, when he was alone praying, the followers came and he asked them, "Who do the people say I am?"

They said, "John the Baptist or Elijah. Some think one of the old prophets has resurrected."

He said, "Who do you think I am?"

Peter answered, "The anointed one from God, Christos."[5]

He warned them not to tell this to anyone. "The son of man has to suffer many things and be censured by the chief priests and experts in the law. He will be killed and then will rise on the third day."

6 Taking up your cross is not just taking on the suffering that comes along with it. It also means going through death experiences. We find a similar theme in Greek spirituality, where Dionysian service means dying through dismemberment and then rising. If we avoid the many kinds of "deaths" that are part of life, we are not taking up the cross.

7 This paradoxical statement is not so unusual in spiritual literature. According to the Tao Te Ching, "Having and not having arise together" (chap. 2). The effort to save your soul—finding a teacher, doing certain things, believing in certain things—may not keep your soul intact. You may have to lose your sense of soul before you can truly have it.

8 In fact, Jesus is giving them a good taste of the kingdom with his way of life: healing, teaching, advocating love and friendship, celebrating life, setting aside strict legalism and judgment.

9 This shamanic vision prepares him for his extraordinarily painful and humiliating death. The cloud is the realm of spirit, a portion of the Father's "sky"; the *mundus imaginalis*, or world of sacred imagination is accessible to everyone, but only if you are free of the anti-imaginal bias of both modernistic philosophies and religious literalism.

10 Fear is an appropriate emotion in this "cloud," because we are now in the presence of a realm entirely different from our usual world and yet profoundly connected to it. Perhaps a more succinct definition of it would be the famous description of the holy from the religion scholar Rudolf Otto: a mystery that is both awe-inspiring and frightening.

11 It is as though the very core of the universe, the voice of life itself, affirms who Jesus is and what he is doing and teaching.

He told them all, "If anyone wants to join me, he has to dis-
regard his own needs and take up his cross every day and follow
me.[6] Whoever wants to save his soul will lose it, but whoever
loses his soul on my behalf will save it.[7] What good is it to
gain the entire world and lose oneself? When the son of man
comes in the splendor of the Father and the holy angels, he will
be embarrassed by anyone who is embarrassed by me and my
teachings. I can assure you that some standing here now will
not taste death until they see the kingdom of God."[8]

About eight days after this, he took Peter, John, and James
with him up a mountain to pray. While he was praying, his face
looked different and his clothes glowed and turned white. Two
men, splendid in appearance, Moses and Elijah, were with him
and were talking about his final leave-taking that he was about
to accomplish in Jerusalem.[9]

Peter and his friends had succumbed to sleep, but when
they woke up they could see his aura and the two men standing beside him. As these two were about to depart, Peter said
to Jesus, "Master, it is good for us to be here. Let's make three
tents: one for you, one for Moses, and one for Elijah." He didn't
know what he was saying.

As he was speaking, a cloud formed and engulfed them.
They were afraid as they entered the cloud.[10] Then a voice
sounded from the cloud, "This is my son, my special one. Heed
him."[11]

After the voice stopped, Jesus was alone.

They kept it all to themselves and spoke to no one about
these events and the things they had seen.

The next day, they came down from the mountain and a
large crowd greeted him. A man from the crowd shouted out,
"Teacher, I beg you to look at my son. He's my only boy."

Suddenly a spirit possessed the boy and he screamed. The
spirit threw him into convulsions and he foamed at the mouth.
It battered him and was reluctant to leave him.

12 Jesus sometimes expresses frustration with people who cannot make the shift to a new way of seeing things. They cannot trust the healing powers of nature or their own power because their vision is limited. Jesus offers a new way of seeing, so he often heals blindness. With a new vision, people could deal with the daimonic, as we could today.

13 You need the perspective of a child—open-minded, adventurous, not calloused or cynical, free to consider radical options. Then, if you welcome Jesus's way into your life, you are welcoming the very heart of being, the fatherly rule of existence.

14 This sentiment—"He isn't one of us"—summarizes an attitude Jesus counters frequently. He himself associates with many different sorts of people and resists being held to conventional standards. He refuses to be put in a single category.

15 This is a line that the religions and spiritual movements of the world could ponder: If you are doing what we do and are not against us, you are one of us. If you are living an intense life of compassion, though you are not an explicit follower of Jesus, you are in the kingdom.

16 Many commentators see the entire Gospel of Luke as having a narrative arc leading to Jerusalem, not just a place but a center and goal of spirituality. Jesus moves toward his death but also his resurrection, to the point where he will be fully present not only as a human with a message but also as a vision to guide humanity toward its fulfillment.

"I begged your followers to get rid of it, but they couldn't do it," the father said.

Jesus said, "You untrusting and confused people. How long do I have to be with you and endure you? Bring your son over here."[12]

As the boy approached, the daimon slammed him to the ground and threw him into a convulsion. Jesus rebuked the unclean spirit, cured the boy, and gave him back to his father. Everyone was stunned at the greatness of God. While they were all marveling at the things going on, Jesus said to the followers, "Listen closely: The son of man is going to be betrayed and delivered into the hands of some men."

They didn't grasp this statement. It was too obscure for them to understand, and they were afraid to ask him about it.

Then an argument arose among them about who among them might be the greatest. Knowing their thoughts, Jesus took a child and placed him at his side.

"Whoever welcomes this child in my name welcomes me, and whoever welcomes me welcomes the one who sent me. Whoever is lowest among you is great."[13]

John said, "Master, we noticed someone expelling daimons in your name, and we tried to stop him since he isn't one of us."[14]

Jesus said, "Don't get in his way. Whoever isn't against you is for you."[15]

The day of Jesus's deliverance was drawing near and he was determined to go to Jerusalem. He sent messengers on ahead, and they traveled and entered a village of Samaritans to make arrangements. But the people there wouldn't agree on a plan, since he was going to Jerusalem.[16] When the followers James and John saw this, they said, "Sir, would you like us to command fire to come down from the sky and destroy them?"

17 In the land of unconsciousness, the default reality, you feel aggression against
those who are not of your circle—in this case, Samaritans. Jesus points out
clearly that this is not the way of the kingdom. Put your aggression away.

18 The implications of Jesus not having a nest or burrow are profound. In the
kingdom, one is a saunterer with no home. In his brilliant comparison of
Jesus and Henry David Thoreau, *Jesus as Precursor*, Robert Funk arrives at the
notion of a shift from sacred precinct to the sacred everywhere. "The wall of
the temenos [boundary of the temple] is broken down; the sacred has come
to dwell in the common and the ordinary."
  —Funk, *Jesus as Precursor* (Missoula, MT: Society of Biblical Literature, 1975),
  102

He looked at them and scolded them, "You don't understand the spirit we're talking about. The son of man didn't come to destroy people but to save them."[17]

They went on to another village. On the road someone told him, "I'll follow you wherever you go."

Jesus said, "The fox has a hole and a bird has a nest, but the son of man doesn't have anywhere to lay his head."[18]

To another person, Jesus said, "Follow me."

But this person responded, "Sir, let me go and bury my father first."

Jesus said to him, "Let the dead bury their dead. But you, you go and announce the kingdom of God everywhere."

Another person said, "I'll follow you, sir, but let me say goodbye to my family first."

Jesus said to him, "You aren't fit for the kingdom of God if, after putting your hand to plow, you look back."

1   To understand this instruction, the words of activist Satish Kumar may help. He describes his early experiences of walking for peace as a Jain monk. His guru told him to walk without money or supplies. "When you have money you can think that money will protect you and support you. But when you have no money you have to trust yourself, you have to trust people, and you have to trust god."
    —Kumar, *Earth Pilgrim* (Totnes, UK: Green Books, 2009), 24

2   You do not have to think of the reference to Sodom as punishment. If any group does not accept the kingdom's vision and values, it will suffer the conflicts and cultural decay that afflict those who live by self-interest and aggression. The arrival of the kingdom points out and roots up corruption.

3   In dealing with the daimonic, it is best not to try to eradicate or dominate it, but to mollify its negative power by forging a workable association. "It is a waste of effort to try to use the daimon as a familiar for one's own purposes; on the contrary, the autonomy of this ambivalent figure should be religiously borne in mind, for it is the source of that fearful power which drives towards individuation. . . . We neither can nor should try to force this numinous being, at the risk of our own psychic destruction, into our narrow human mold, for it is greater than man's consciousness and greater than his will."
    —C. G. Jung, "Alchemical Studies," in *Collected Works of C. G. Jung*, vol. 13, translated by R. F. C. Hull (Princeton, NJ: Princeton University Press, 1967), sec. 437

Chapter 10

Then the master selected seventy people and dispatched them ahead of him in pairs to every town and area he planned on visiting. He told them, "The harvest is bountiful but the workers are few. So ask the master of the harvest to get more workers for the harvest. Get going. See, I'm sending you out like lambs among wolves. Don't take a money bag or sandals. Don't say hello to anyone on the road.[1]

"When you enter a house, say, 'May peace be in this house.' If someone there is interested in peace, your expression of peace will have a response. If not, you will still have your peace. Stay in that house, eating and drinking whatever they offer, because a worker deserves some kind of pay. Don't go from house to house.

"Whenever you come into a town and its people welcome you, eat what they offer you. Care for the sick there and tell them that the kingdom of God has come. But if a town doesn't welcome you, step into the street and shout, 'In protest we shake off the very dirt on our feet that has come from your town.' Be aware. The kingdom of God is very close. I'm sorry, but on that very day it would be better for Sodom than for that town.[2]

"Too bad, Chorazin. Too bad, Bethsaida. If the displays of power done for you had been done for Tyre and Sidon, they would have changed their ways a long time ago. At the judgment, it will be easier for them than it will be for you. And you, Capernaum. Will you be lifted up to the sky? No, you'll be sent down to Hades.

"Whoever hears you, hears me. Whoever rejects you, rejects me. Whoever rejects me, rejects the one who sent me."

The seventy people came back happy. "Sir," they said, "in your name the daimons aligned with us."[3]

4   Jung offers this same advice: Do not become so filled with your own sense of importance when you discover that you have some power in relation to the daimon. Rather appreciate that you have an effective connection with the realm of the sky, the Father, the spirit.

5   Earth and sky—a key theme in the Gospels. As alchemists would say later, "As above, so below." Always live in these two dimensions: the spiritual and the earthly. In the text we often see the word *ouranos* for the sky and *ge* for the earth: two Greek deities and mysteries that are relevant to us today, archetypal dimensions that we have to deal with every day.

6   Each human being has certain strengths, talents, education, and calling. Not everyone can be an intermediary with the realm of spirit. Jesus is something of a shaman in this respect, able to connect earth and sky, or ordinary life and spirit. In him you meet the great Father spirit that sustains life.

7   In Greek, *zoen aionion*. Think of "zoo," the strangeness, beauty, and great range of life, and "aion," a Mithraic figure, a man with a lion's head, encircled by a snake, holding the keys to the past and the future. Often translated as "eternal life," it may mean not only unending life but also life outside the materialistic limits of modern understanding, where visions and miracles and healings and resurrections are a natural occurrence—outside of time, not just endless time. See Jung, "The Symbolic Life," in *Collected Works*, vol. 18, sec. 266.

8   To be free of the shackles of time-bound life, secularism, all you have to do is love with your whole being, loving yourself and the other. Love is not just an emotion but a way of being connected and open to the world in its fullness.

9   The kingdom intensifies life. Jesus refers to himself as life. The point is not to know and understand or to change or to believe. It is to have more life—to enjoy an intense presence and engagement, not to be blocked by narcissism and paranoia, which are widespread obstacles to vitality and connection.

He said, "I watched Satan fall from the sky like a bolt of lightning. You see, I gave you the authority to step on snakes and scorpions. I gave you power over the enemy. Nothing can harm you. But don't get inflated about the fact that spirits submit to you. Rather, enjoy the fact that your names are written in the sky."[4]

Jesus felt profound joy in the Holy Spirit and said, "I celebrate you, Father, Lord of earth and sky.[5] You've kept these matters from the wise and educated and revealed them to children. Yes, Father, this plan pleases you. My Father has given me everything. No one knows about the son except the Father, or who the Father is except the son and anyone to whom the son wants to make him known."[6]

To his followers he said privately, "Fortunate are the eyes that see what you see. Many kings and prophets would like to have seen the things you've seen and didn't see them, and to hear the things you've heard and didn't hear them.

A legal expert came forward to test Jesus. "Teacher, what do I need to do to inherit timeless life?"[7]

Jesus said, "What do you find written in the law? How do you understand it?"

He said, "Love the Lord your God with all your heart and soul and power and intelligence. Love your neighbor as yourself."[8]

Jesus said, "You're right. Do this and you will be alive."[9]

10 Some say that the priest and Levite would not break the purification laws by approaching an injured foreigner. But the Samaritan, too, perhaps, was guided by similar laws. In this interpretation, he knows when to break a rule to do good. This reading implies that to be in the kingdom you honor rules of society and religion but know when to break them. See Raj Nadella, *Dialogue, Not Dogma: Many Voices in the Gospel of Luke* (New York: Bloomsbury, 2011), 80.

11 Not just a moral or exemplary tale, this beloved story, which is unique to the Book of Luke, picks up the theme of the outsider. Insiders tend to think of their group as morally and ethically superior. They may consider others insensitive and immoral. This is not just a judgment but also a profound archetypal pattern. This story makes us reflect on our unconscious assumptions about being on the side of good. Feeling virtuous and right may blind us to the ethical demands of actual life.

12 "Jesus was defending the woman who would be criticized in his era for acting outside her condoned space, entering the world of the learned (signified by sitting at the feet of a teacher). So, far from closing women into a safe retreat from the world, he was beckoning them out into it, to join men in knowledge and action."
—Garry Wills, *What Jesus Meant* (New York: Viking, 2006), 49

Wishing to show that he was a decent man, he said to Jesus, "Who is my neighbor?"

Jesus responded. "A man was traveling from Jerusalem to Jericho and ran into robbers. They tore off his clothes and beat him up. Then they left him for dead. A priest happened to be walking down that road and saw him and passed by on the other side. A Levite, too, when he got there and saw him, passed by on the other side. But a Samaritan on a trip came along and felt compassion for him.[10] He bandaged his wounds and rubbed oil and wine on them, put him on his donkey, took him to a hotel, and took care of him.

"The next day the Samaritan gave the innkeeper two denarii and said, 'Take care of him. If it costs more money, I'll repay you when I get back.'

"Which of the three do you think was a neighbor to the man who ran into robbers?"

The man said, "The person who was kind to him."

Jesus said, "All right. Go and do likewise."[11]

As they were traveling, he came to a village, where a woman named Martha welcomed him into her home. She had a sister, Mary, who sat at the master's feet, listening to his every word. Martha was distracted by all her housework. She said to Jesus, "Sir, doesn't it bother you that my sister has left me to do all the work? Tell her to help me."

The master answered, "Martha, Martha, you're anxious about many things, but only one thing is essential. Mary has chosen the better part, and I won't take that away from her."[12]

1   You keep the name "God" sacred by not limiting it or pretending to know
    what it means. "God" is a mystery, and it takes circumspection to keep it
    sacred. The prayer begins with this wish because everything else depends
    on it. Not keeping the name of God sacred is the fundamental problem of
    religion in our time.

2   Everything Jesus says or does is intended to create a higher level of human
    existence, one at peace, built on radical forgiveness, and energized by love.
    The metaphor for this new condition for humanity is the kingdom of God,
    or of the sky. It is embodied in a church only to the extent that the members
    actually achieve a high degree of vitality through radical love.

3   "The ability to forgive is clearly not just one of several items in a repertoire
    of qualities desirable in a follower of Jesus. It is rather an absolutely nec-
    essary dimension of Christian existence, as eschatological existence in the
    end-time community. . . . There can be no 'bread of life' unless there is also
    forgiveness."
        —George M. Soares-Prabhu, *The Dharma of Jesus*, edited by Francis X. D'Sa
        (Maryknoll, NY: Orbis Books, 2003), 222

4   This is not a spirituality of passive petitions. Action, persistence, and expec-
    tation are important, because living a good life on earth is important. There
    is a constant interchange between "the man behind the door" and the aver-
    age person trying to make a good life. Here Jesus adds persistence as a virtue
    in his way of life.

5   Jesus urges us to dialogue with the fatherly aspect of life, that which gives us
    what we need to thrive. This dialogue is a form of prayer, available to any-
    one, in which we express our need. It is not based on a naive expectation that
    life will miraculously offer something good for us, but on our responsibility
    to acknowledge our dependence and to trust in spite of losses and needs.

Chapter 11

O ne day Jesus was praying. When he was done, a follower asked him, "Would you teach us how to pray, the way John taught his followers?"

He said, "When you pray, say this:

> *Father,*
> *May your name be kept sacred.*[1]
> *May your kingdom become a reality.*[2]
> *Every day give us the bread we need for that day.*
> *Forgive us our wrongdoing,*
> *As we forgive anyone who has done anything to us.*[3]
> *And free us from the things that seduce us."*

Then he said, "Suppose you have a friend and go to him in the middle of the night and say, 'Friend, could you lend me three loaves of bread? A friend of mine is on a trip and has come to my place, and I have nothing to offer him.'

"Suppose he answers from inside his house, 'Don't bother me. My house is shut up and my children and I are in bed. I can't get up and give you anything.'

"I assure you, he may not get up and give you something because of your friendship, but because of the persistence of the one asking he will get up and give you whatever you need.

"So I say, ask and you'll be given something. Look and you'll find something. Knock and a door will open for you.[4]

"Suppose a child asks his father for a fish. Would he hand him a snake? If the child asks for an egg, would he give him a scorpion? If you, not exactly perfect, know enough to give good things to your children, how much more likely will your Father above give a holy spirit to those who ask?"[5]

6   Let's not think of the cures and exorcisms as mere displays of power, but signs and metaphors as well. An unclean spirit, or daimon, can take away the power of our words. Unresolved anger, xenophobia, prejudice, or narcissistic greed are all signs of a daimonic possession. We cannot speak our truth when we're overwhelmed by these impulses. In some ways we are mute and need a cleansing in order to speak effectively. This can happen to any of us at any time.

7   You do not get rid of what possesses you by dark exorcisms but by the values of the kingdom—forgiveness, love, friendship, and a desire to heal. The daimon today may be experienced as an addiction. To get rid of it, you need a renewal of self, including the actions mentioned. You have to live with an open heart and with the courage to do good. In this way the kingdom, with its set of visionary values, relieves you of your daimons.

8   There is no middle ground between being a kind, healing person and a self-absorbed, angry, and divisive one. By your decision about how to live you are either rescued from a purposeless life or given a purpose. Citizens of the kingdom are self-selected by the way they imagine life and by how they live.

9   Traditionally, an unclean spirit seeks out a desert or a dry place. This makes sense; unclean spirits make us dry—desiccated, emotionless, and unengaged.

Once he was expelling a daimon from a man who couldn't talk. When the daimon had gone, the man spoke, and the people were astonished. But some said, "He expels daimons by Beelzeboul, the ruler of daimons."[6]

Others wanted to test him and demanded an omen in the sky. But he knew what they had in mind and said, "Any kingdom that is polarized is worthless. A house divided against itself can't survive. If Satan is divided against himself, how can his kingdom remain? You're saying that I expel daimons by Beelzeboul, but if I get rid of daimons by Beelzeboul, by whom do your children expel them? Let them be your criteria. If, however, I expel daimons by the finger of God, then the kingdom has come to you.[7]

"When a tough man, heavily armed, guards his house, his things go untouched. But when a stronger person attacks and overpowers him, he snatches up all the armor the man had relied on and distributes the booty.

"Whoever is not with me is against me, and whoever does not join me is out on his own.[8]

"When an unclean spirit comes out of a person, it wanders through arid places[9] looking for peace. Not finding it, it thinks, 'I'll go back to the house where I came from.' Then, when it comes, it finds it swept up and put in order. It picks up seven more spirits, worse than itself, and they enter and take up residence. The last condition of the person is worse than the first."

10 A basic teaching in this Gospel: Hear the word and then act on it. Listening closely and then living accordingly are like one whole—two sides of the one action.

11 In the gospel, Jonah is an image looking ahead to Jesus being dead and then rising. But Jonah is also an image of the "Night Sea Journey," the rite of passage in which a person feels captive in a dark night and then emerges like a new person. Joseph Campbell describes this within the context of the hero's journey: "Allegorically, then, the passage into a temple and the hero-dive through the haws of the whale are identical adventures, both denoting, in picture language, the life-centering, life-renewing act."
—Campbell, *The Hero with a Thousand Faces* (New York: MJF Books, 1949), 92

12 "Because he [Jesus] is greater than Job, greater than Jonah, the Job and Jonah rites of passage will enact themselves more comprehensively and more inwardly in him."
—John Moriarty, *Dreamtime* (Dublin: Lilliput Press, 1999), 42

13 In chapter 8 there is a similar instruction, and both instances show a subtle psychological point: When you live your life according to Jesus's teachings, you develop an inner luminosity that inspires others and rewards you with a personal clarity. There are no dark places in you to cause worry or low self-esteem.

14 Here Jesus clearly indicates how much he is interested in the inner life, the soul; not just external behavior, but also who you are as a person. External rituals can be effective, but only if they speak to and foster a rich inner life. Those who go to church, temple, or mosque without an active inner motivation risk being outside the kingdom. That would be a tragedy, because only in the kingdom do we discover and develop our humanity.

While Jesus was speaking, a woman in the crowd raised her voice and said, "Blessed is the womb that bore you and the breasts that nursed you."

He replied, "No, blessed are those who hear the word of God and act on it."[10]

The crowds were getting larger. He said, "This is a wicked generation. It wants a model, but no model will be given except the image of Jonah. Just as Jonah was a model for the Ninevites, so will the son of man be for this generation.[11]

"The Queen of the South will come forward with the people of this generation at the judgment and condemn them. She came from the far corners of the world to hear Solomon's wisdom, and look, something greater than Solomon is here.

"The men of Nineveh will stand with this generation at the judgment and condemn it. When Jonah appealed to them, they changed at heart, but something greater than Jonah is here now.[12]

"No one lights a lamp and then puts it in the basement or under a bowl.[13] You put it on a stand so that anyone present might see the light. Your eye is the lamp of your body. When it's clear, your whole body is full of light and has no dark places. It glows brilliantly, the way a lamp illumines you with its rays."

When he finished speaking, a Pharisee invited Jesus to lunch. So he went and sat at the table. The Pharisee watched him and was surprised that he didn't ritually wash before the meal. The master told him, "You Pharisees clean the outside of the cup and dish, but inside you're filled with larceny and wickedness. You're foolish. Didn't he who made the outside make the inside as well?[14] If you give from within with love, then everything about you will be clean.

15 Sophia is the eternal wisdom, the law of life and a human being's perception of that law. She is described beautifully in the Hebrew Bible's book of Sirach 24:28–32: "The first human being ever created never knew Wisdom completely, and the last person on earth will be no more successful. The possibilities of Wisdom are vaster than the ocean; her resources are more profound than the deepest waters beneath the earth. As for me, I thought of myself as an irrigation canal bringing water from a river into a garden. I only intended to water my orchard and flowerbeds, but the canal soon became a river, and the river became a sea. And so I present you with my learning; I hold it high, so that its light can be seen everywhere, like that of the rising sun" (Good News Translation).

16 These are the religious legalists, who are still among us, telling us what to believe and how to carry out our spiritual inclinations. Rules have a place in a spiritual community, mainly for preserving the initial inspiration and teachings, but they can easily become a burden, getting in the way of a person's own inspiration and intelligence. This legalistic impulse may also be a subtle influence *inside* us, in our thoughts and fantasies.

"Be careful, Pharisees. You give a portion of mint and rue and all kinds of garden herbs as a tithe, but you pay no attention to issues of justice and the love of God. You should do these things as well as the others.

"Be careful, Pharisees. You like the top seats in the synagogues and respect in the marketplace.

"Be careful. You're like cemetery plots that people walk over without realizing it."

A lawyer responded to him, "Teacher, when you talk like this, you're insulting us, too."

He said, "Lawyers, too, be careful. You crush people with burdens difficult to bear but then don't lift a finger to help.

"Be careful. You make monuments for the prophets, but it was your fathers who killed them. You acknowledge and approve the actions of your fathers. They killed the prophets and you build the monuments.

"This is why Sophia, God in his Wisdom,[15] said, 'I send them prophets and apostles. Some they kill and some they prosecute. The blood of all the prophets, shed since the beginning of the world, is on the hands of this generation. From Abel to Zechariah, who was killed between the altar and the house of God, I'm telling you, their blood is on the hands of this generation.'

"Be careful, lawyers. You have stolen the key to knowledge. You didn't enter the place of knowledge yourselves and you stood in the way of those who were trying to enter."[16]

As Jesus was leaving that place, the experts in the law and the Pharisees became antagonistic and interrogated him closely on many topics, scheming and hoping to catch him up in something he might say.

1   In the kingdom, the individual counts. No matter how many people are
    in a community, their individual needs, talents, and voice are significant.
    Religious institutions are often tempted to repress the individual, creating a
    separation between leadership and the masses.

2   Rather than think of the "Holy Spirit" as a dove or a phantasm somewhere,
    you might consider it less physically as the spirit of holiness that you sense
    around certain people or in certain places and situations. Taking this spirit
    seriously, fostering it, and keeping it intact are essential for human life, more
    essential than the person of Jesus, according to this passage.

Chapter 12

A crowd of thousands had come together, so packed that they were stepping all over each other. Jesus spoke to his followers first.

"Be cautious around the 'yeast' of the Pharisees, their hypocrisy. There is nothing hidden now that won't be uncovered, nothing concealed that won't be revealed. So, whatever you've uttered in darkness will be heard in the light of day, and whatever you've whispered in back rooms will be shouted from rooftops. I beg you, friends, don't be afraid of anyone who kills the body and can do no other harm. But I do warn you about someone who, once he has killed, has the power to toss you into the abyss. Yes, be afraid of him.

"Don't they sell five sparrows for two cents? Yet God is aware of each one of them. In fact, the very hairs of your head are all numbered. So don't be afraid. You're worth much more than many sparrows.[1]

"I assure you, anyone who speaks out for me in the presence of human beings, the son of man will speak for in the presence of God's angels. Whoever ignores me in the presence of human beings will be ignored in the presence of God's angels.

"Anyone who speaks against the son of man will find forgiveness, but whoever dishonors the Holy Spirit will never find forgiveness.[2]

"When they bring you up before the leaders and authorities in the synagogues, don't be concerned about how to speak or what to say in your defense. The Holy Spirit will coach you at that time about what to say."

A person in the crowd said, "Teacher, tell my brother to share the family inheritance with me."

3   We might take this parable to heart in relation to our national, family, and personal treasuries. Rather than measure wealth by the visible things we own, we might measure it in invisible things of the spirit and soul. How much love do you have in your life? Friendship? Ideas? Service? Animal life? Nature?

4   "A Zen line in Job: 'Is it by your wisdom that the hawk soars?' (39:26)."
    —Thomas Merton, *Conjectures of a Guilty Bystander* (New York: Doubleday, 1989), 285

5   Some religious people promote the idea that we should not worry about poverty and hunger in the world. God will provide. But that interpretation misses the next line about the kingdom. Yes, from a certain point of view the values of the kingdom are more important than worries about possessions. But in the kingdom one does indeed feed the hungry and help the poor.

Jesus answered, "Sir, who made me a judge or mediator for you? Be careful. Watch out for any form of greed. If you have a lot of property, your life may be all about your possessions."

He told them a parable: "A wealthy man had some very productive land, and he thought, 'What am I going to do? I have no place to store my crops. I know, I'll take my barns down and build bigger ones and store all my grain and goods in them. I'll say to my soul, "Soul, you have plenty of things stored up for years to come. Take it easy. Eat, drink, and be happy.'"

"But God told him, 'You're a fool. This very night your soul may be taken. Now who will own what you have acquired?' This person has stored up possessions for himself but is not wealthy in the things of God."[3]

He told his followers, "This is why I tell you, don't worry about how you'll get food to stay alive or how you'll clothe your body. Life is far more than food and the body far more than clothes. Consider the ravens. They don't plant or harvest. They have no storerooms or barns. Yet God feeds them.[4] How much more important are you than birds? Who can add an hour to his life by worrying? If you can't do these little things, why worry about other things?

"Consider the lilies of the field. Notice how they grow. They don't work hard or weave. But not even Solomon in all his glory was dressed like one of these. If God clothes the grass that is green today but tomorrow goes into the furnace, how much more will he clothe you. You people are lacking in trust. Don't keep worrying about what to eat and drink. People all over the world are always looking for these things, but the Father knows what you need. Keep your eye on his kingdom and you'll have everything.[5]

6   "I have never been in any rich man's house which would not have looked
    the better for having a bonfire made outside of it of nine-tenths of all that
    it held."
        —William Morris, *Collected Works of William Morris*, vol. 22 (Cambridge, UK:
        Cambridge University Press, 2012), 48

7   A common understanding of this preparation for the coming of the son is
    the destruction of the world. A deeper interpretation might be the decon-
    struction of the world as we know it with its moral and scientific certain-
    ties. That materialistic, rationalistic world collapses all the time. It fails us
    as human beings. Jesus presents a new reality in the notion of the kingdom
    above. The sky is the metaphor, the reality is a style of living that is higher
    in meaning and moral sensitivity. We must be ready at all times for the con-
    tinuous collapse of the old reality. See Robert Funk, *A Credible Jesus: Fragments
    of a Vision* (Santa Rosa, CA: Polebridge Press, 2002), 148.

"Don't be afraid, little flock, the Father has graciously decided to give you the kingdom.

"Sell your possessions and give to charity. Make purses that don't wear out. Store up a treasure in the sky, where a thief can't cause trouble or a moth destroy. Where your treasure lies, that is where you heart will be.[6]

"Be prepared. Have your clothes on. Keep your lamps lit. Be like people waiting for the master to come back from the wedding party so they can open the door for him right away when he comes and knocks. Blessed are the servants the master finds ready when he arrives. He will be dressed to serve and ask them to sit at the table and he will be there to wait on them. Whether he comes in the second watch or the third and finds them ready, blessed are those servants. You can be certain that if the head of the house knew when the thief was coming, he would not let his house be broken into. You should be ready, too, because the son of man is coming at a time you won't expect."[7]

Peter asked, "Sir, are you telling this parable for us or everyone else as well?"

The master said, "Who is the faithful and trusted steward the master will place in charge of his servants to feed them at the appropriate times? Blessed is that servant the master finds doing this when he arrives. He'll give him authority over all his possessions.

"But if this servant thinks, 'The master won't be here for a long time,' and beats the servants, men and women, and eats and drinks and gets drunk, the master may come in unexpectedly and will remove him and put him among the faithless ones. That servant, who understood what his master wanted but didn't get ready and do what was required, will be beaten. The one who didn't know and did what deserved a beating will be given a light penalty. If you have been given a lot, a lot will be asked of you. If a lot has been entrusted to you, more will be demanded.

8 Jesus's words have heat in them, a heat that could transform sluggish, default life into intensified and spiritually invigorated life.

9 There will be little agreement about the radical proposal Jesus makes for a lifestyle where possessions are an obstacle: You are supposed to love your neighbors and your enemies, and rules are meant to be broken in the name of care and love.

10 Make a personal moral decision rather than waiting for someone else to frame it as a law or a rule. The kingdom is less legalistic and more moral than most of society.

"I came to bring fire to the earth and wish it were now ablaze.[8] I have a baptism to go through, and I am anxious until it is finished. Do you think I have come to bring harmony to the earth? No, I'm here to bring discord. Five people in a household will be divided: two against three, three against two. Father against son, son against father; mother against daughter, daughter against mother; mother-in-law against daughter-in-law, daughter-in-law against mother-in-law.[9]

"When you see a cloud rising in the west, you think, 'It's going to rain.' And it happens. When you see the south wind blow, you think, 'It's going to be a hot one.' And it happens. You're hypocrites. You know how to interpret signs in the earth and sky, but not the times we're in.

"Why not make your own decisions about what is right? Say you go with your accuser before a judge. On the way over, try to settle the issue. Otherwise, you may be dragged before the judge, who will hand you over to a bailiff, and the bailiff will toss you in jail. You won't get out until you've paid the last penny."[10]

1 This theme of a physical versus a meaningful universe comes up frequently
   in the Gospels. Which is more calamitous—to have a tower fall on your
   head or to live an unconscious, materialistic, and narcissistic life? Jesus nom-
   inates the latter as a bigger problem.

2 Here we learn how to act in the kingdom: You care for life and do not give
   up on it. Figuratively, you apply manure and the plant may thrive. We need
   to spread manure on our lives as well. Find those things that foster a soulful
   life and be patient with your care.

Chapter 13

People with Jesus told him about some Galileans whose blood Pilate had mixed in with their sacrifices.

Jesus said, "Do you think that these Galileans were worse people because they suffered this way? I would say no. Unless you have a profound change of heart, you will all suffer the way they did. What about the eighteen people who were killed when the tower at Siloam fell on them? Do you think they were worse than anyone else living in Jerusalem? I would say no. Unless you have a profound change of heart, you will all suffer the way they did."[1]

Then he told a parable: "A man planted a fig tree in his vineyard. One day he looked for some fruit on it and didn't find any. He spoke to the farmer. 'For three years I've been waiting for fruit to appear on this fig tree, but so far nothing. Cut it down. It's just wasting good soil.'

"The man responded, 'Sir, let it go for another year. I'll dig up the earth around it and mix some manure in. If it bears fruit next year, great. If not, let's cut it down.'"[2]

3   We have seen how blindness is not just physical but also moral. Here the problem is being stooped over and becoming straight. This may imply that we need to be healed of our excessive meekness and instead stand upright, strong and prepared for anything. This personal forcefulness is a point of character in the kingdom.

4   Being in the kingdom involves a different way of thinking. Many have been raised to believe that if you follow the rules, you are a good person and on the proper side. But Jesus challenges that deep-seated concept. Sometimes you must break the rules in the name of human compassion.

5   From a certain point of view, being in the kingdom is a small thing, a different perspective on life, a slight shift in the way you imagine things. But this slight shift, *metanoia*, accounts for a serious change in character. That change makes you fit for the kingdom.

6   "Sufism is a leaven [yeast] within all human society . . . an adventure, a goal of human perfection attained by reviewing and awakening within humanity a higher organ of fulfillment, completion, destiny."
    —Idries Shah, *The Sufis* (New York: Anchor Books, 1971), 56

7   In the Gospels we are told to take the narrow road, go through the eye of a needle, and, now, use the narrow door. Choosing the kingdom is not the easy way, but it is the way in which you become fully human and fully yourself.

Jesus was teaching in a synagogue on the Sabbath when a woman showed up who had been disabled for eighteen years by a spirit. She was bent over and couldn't stand up straight. When Jesus saw her, he called her over and said, "Woman, you are now free of your condition." Her put his hand on her and instantly she stood up straight and praised God.[3]

But the leader of the synagogue was upset that Jesus had tended someone on the Sabbath and said to the people, "Work may be done on six days. Come on those days for treatment, but not on the Sabbath. The master replied, "You're hypocrites. On the Sabbath don't you all untie your ox or donkey from the feeding trough and lead it to water? Shouldn't this woman, bound by Satan for eighteen long years, be set free from her travail on the Sabbath?"[4]

When he spoke, his adversaries were shamed and the crowd thrilled at the wonderful things he had done.

He spoke again. "What is the kingdom of God like? Is there something I can compare it to? It's like a mustard seed that a person planted in a garden. It grew into a tree and birds made nests in its branches.[5] It's like yeast that a woman mixed with three measures, or twenty-two liters, of flour until all of it rose."[6]

On his way to Jerusalem, Jesus went through town after town, teaching. Someone asked, "Sir, will only some be saved?"

He said, "Make an effort to go through the narrow door. Many will try that but will fail.[7]

"When the owner of a house gets up and closes his door and you're outside, knocking and saying, 'Sir, please open up,' he'll say, 'I don't know where you've come from.'

"You'll say, 'We ate and drank with you. You were teaching in our neighborhoods.'

8   This is a warning to all of us. We pray to God, thinking we know who God
    is. We have many ideas about him—to even refer to him as *him* is question-
    able. When we knock on his door, he may not recognize us because we may
    have all the wrong ideas. Our heroes, our prophets, may not be his. And so
    we need an absolutely open mind about the object of our faith and devotion.
    We cannot be absolute in our attachment to traditions and creeds.

9   An interesting image for Jesus. Here, not the Good Shepherd but the hen
    who shields her young under her wings. Fourteenth-century mystic Julian
    of Norwich writes: "Jesus Christ therefore, who himself overcame evil with
    good, is our true Mother. We received our 'Being' from Him and this is where
    His Maternity starts. And with it comes the gentle Protection and Guard of
    Love which will never cease to surround us."
    —Julian of Norwich (1342–1416), *Revelations of Divine Love*, LIX.

"But he'll answer, 'I really don't know where you have come from. Go away, all you bad people.' When you see Abraham and Isaac and Jacob and all the prophets, you'll be removed to a place where there is wailing and teeth-clenching. People will come from the east and the west, from north and south, and will feast in the kingdom of God. In fact, the last will be first and the first last."[8]

About then some Pharisees arrived on the scene and said, "Get away from here. Herod wants to kill you."

He said, "Go and tell that fox, 'Notice, I'm expelling daimons and healing today and tomorrow, and on the third day I complete my activity. And yet, today, tomorrow, and the third day I have to be going. A prophet can't be killed outside of Jerusalem. Yes, Jerusalem, Jerusalem. The city that murders prophets and stones people sent there. Often I have wanted to gather your children together as a hen shields her young under her wings.[9] But you were not willing. Your house is abandoned. You won't see me again until the day when people say, 'Blessed is he who comes in the name of the Lord.'"

1   Notice this dinner with a leader of the Pharisees. In doing his work, Jesus teaches, heals, prays, and has dinner with all sorts of people. This interesting mode of creating a new world could be part of our practice today.

2   Surely these examples are not just meant to tell us how to act in public. At a deeper level and on a larger scale they describe how things work in the kingdom. You do not find "success," whatever that means, through literal prestige but paradoxically through genuine humility. The kingdom is an upside-down world, not unlike that of the Chinese Tao Te Ching, where you read: "Give up sainthood, renounce wisdom, and it will be a hundred times better for everyone."
    —Tao Te Ching, translated by Gia-Fu Feng and Jane English (New York: Vintage Books, 1972), 19

3   Remember that this is a parable. The point is, do not look for human logic and human emotional and physical rewards. The poor will not give you more money, but they will give you the character you need to be a citizen of the kingdom of the sky, or a follower of God. It is a more elevated system of values. Justice is a major element, so the parable ends by suggesting that the right way of living leads not to literal wealth but to the reward of justice, which hopefully one day will be humanity's fate.

Chapter 14

One time Jesus went to the home of a leader of the Pharisees to have dinner on the Sabbath.[1] They were keeping an eye on him. But a man came along who had dropsy. Jesus asked the lawyers and the Pharisees, "Is it legal to treat people on the Sabbath?"

They didn't say anything. So Jesus healed the man and sent him off.

Jesus said, "If one of you had an ox or a donkey that fell into a well, wouldn't you pull it out on the Sabbath?"

They didn't know what to say.

When he noticed at dinner how guests selected certain places of honor, he told them a parable:

"When someone invites you to a wedding party, don't sit down at the place of honor. Someone more distinguished than you may show up. The host who asked both of you may come and tell you, 'Would you please give your place to this person?' No, when you're invited, go and sit in the least conspicuous place. Then, when the host comes, he may tell you, 'Friend, I have a better seat for you.' Everyone at the table will honor you that way. Anyone who gives himself high honors will be humbled, and anyone who is humble will be given honor."[2]

He said to his host, "When you give a luncheon or dinner, don't invite friends, brothers, relatives, or wealthy neighbors. They may invite you in return and you'll have a reward. When you give a dinner, invite the poor, the disabled, the weak, and the blind. Since they can't repay you, you will have a reward at the restoration of the kingdom."[3]

Hearing this, one of the dinner guests said, "Blessed is anyone who eats bread in the kingdom of God."

4 The religions get it wrong when they focus on membership, rather than reaching out to everyone with their treasuries of wisdom. The person who thinks he is virtuous for believing a certain way or is part of a select group is in for a surprise. The average person on the street has a better chance of being part of the kingdom. That sense of self-satisfied virtue and spiritual privilege is an obstacle to the Jesus way.

5 This is another teaching that is difficult to understand at face value. Most people probably have to go their own way, which may contradict the thinking and values of their family. You enter the kingdom with a new and fresh vision, not with the old, regimented ways. Your own way also includes your own form of challenge and suffering.

6 Most people do not think through their choice of spiritual path. Many just repeat what they saw in their families or are drawn in a certain direction emotionally. Jesus here recommends thought and preparation.

7 The point of this parable is rather subtle. If you want to be a citizen of the kingdom, which is the same, of course, as following Jesus, you must be prepared. You cannot be focused on material rewards in life. You must look more deeply and live on a higher spiritual plane. If you are not preoccupied with material gains, then you have a good chance to live the special life and share the vision of the kingdom.

Jesus responded, "Someone once gave a grand dinner and invited a lot of people. When the date for the dinner came, he sent servants to the invitees to tell them to come: 'Everything is ready.' But they all made their excuses. 'I just bought a piece of land and have to inspect it. Sorry.' 'I just bought five teams of oxen. Can't make it.' 'I just got married and can't come.' The servant returned and told his master what happened. The master got angry. 'All right,' he said. 'Go into the streets and lanes of the town and bring the poor, the disabled, the blind, and the sick.' Later, the servant said, 'We did what you asked, but there is still room.'

"The master said, 'Well then, go out to the roads and paths and urge people to come, so that my house will be filled. I'm telling you, none of those who were invited will have a bite of this dinner.'"[4]

Facing the large crowds, Jesus said, "Whoever comes to me and doesn't reject his father and mother, his wife and children, his brothers and sisters, and life itself can't be my disciple. And whoever doesn't carry his cross and follow me can't be my disciple.[5]

"Who starts to build a tower without first sitting down and considering the cost, to see whether he has the resources to complete it? Otherwise, after laying a foundation and not being able to finish the job, people will laugh at him. They'll say, 'This fellow began to build and couldn't finish.'[6]

"What king about to wage war with another king doesn't sit down first and consider whether he can fight the other's twenty thousand men with his ten thousand? If he can't, then when the other is still far away, he will send a delegation and ask for terms of peace. The point is, none of you can be my disciple if you don't give away all your possessions.[7]

8 Now we can add salt to our list of images for the way the kingdom intensifies life. Others were yeast, wine, fire, baptismal water, and oil. Salt offers
   intensity, endurance, and effectiveness. Jesus's teaching is like salt in that it
   brings fervor to life and helps us remain steadfast and true.

"Salt is great, but if salt has lost its tang, how can its saltiness come back? It's not good for the soil or for the manure heap. Throw it away. If you're not deaf, listen."[8]

1   It is more important to bring a lost soul into the kingdom than to worry about people already inclined in that direction and whose lives are quite good. Jesus's compassion focuses on the lost ones, those among us caught up in distractions that blind them and cause them to waste their lives.

2   The legalists don't like Jesus associating with outcasts, but the angels celebrate the outcasts found and transformed.

3   These parables, of course, are all about *metanoia*, and the word is used explicitly. John Dominic Crossan adds an interesting point: "If Jesus and/or God could be the Good Shepherd of the first story in Luke 15:3–7, why not also the Good Housewife of Luke 15:8–10?"
    —Crossan, *The Dark Interval: Towards a Theology of Story* (Santa Rosa, CA: Polebridge Press, 1988), 79.

Chapter 15

Revenue clerks and riffraff were coming together to listen to Jesus. So the Pharisees and law teachers were saying, "This man welcomes misfits and even eats with them."

So Jesus told them this parable: "Suppose you have one hundred sheep and you lose one of them. Do you leave ninety-nine out in the open and search for the lost sheep until you find it? Then, when you find it, do you happily put it on your shoulders and go home? Do you call your friends and neighbors together and say, 'Celebrate with me; I've found my lost sheep'? In the same way, there is more happiness in the heavens about one lost soul who has a change of heart than over ninety-nine good people who don't need to change.[1]

"Let's say a woman has ten silver coins and loses one. Won't she light a lamp, sweep the house, and look everywhere until she finds it? When she finally finds it, she'll notify her friends and neighbors and say, 'Celebrate with me. I found my lost coin.' In the same way, there is happiness among God's angels[2] over one lost soul who has a change of heart."[3]

4 The parable of the prodigal son is a powerful story that is also unique to Luke.

5 Here is the key: He came to himself. He had a change of mind and heart. *Metanoia*, the most important development in a person's life. You stop acting out. You become a person again, thinking and reflecting. You see what you are doing and decide to change.

Jesus went on, "A man had two sons.[4] The younger one said to his father, 'Father, give me my share of the property that will be mine.' So the man divided his property between his sons. A few days later, the younger son got together everything that was his and went off to another country. There he squandered his property in wild living. When it was all gone, a terrible famine struck that area and suddenly the young man was in great need. A citizen of that country hired him to go out into the fields and feed the pigs. He would have been happy to stuff himself with the husks the pigs were eating, since no one gave him anything. But then he came to himself[5] and thought, 'How many of my father's workers have as much bread as they need, and here I am dying from hunger. I'll get up and go to my father and tell him, 'Father, I have done a terrible thing, offending both you and the heavens. I'm no longer worthy to be called your son. Treat me like one of your workers.' Indeed, he went off to his father.

"He was still a ways off when his father saw him and was filled with compassion. He ran and put his arms around him and kissed him. Then the son said, 'Father, I have done a terrible thing in your eyes and before the heavens. I am no longer worthy to be called your son.'

"But the father said to the servants, 'Quick. Bring out a coat. The best one. Put it on him. Put a ring on his finger and sandals on his feet. Get the well-fed calf and slaughter it. Let's eat and celebrate. My son was dead and has come back to life. He was lost and has been found.' They did indeed celebrate.

"The older son was in a field, and when he came toward the house he heard music and dancing. He called one of the servants and asked what was going on. 'Your brother has come back, and your father has slaughtered the well-fed calf because he has him back safely.'

6 This is a subtle story. The brother who did everything right does not get a party, but the one who did everything wrong gets a warm and lavish welcome. Could Oscar Wilde be right when he says, "Christ, through some divine instinct in him, seems to have always loved the sinner as being the nearest possible approach to the perfection of man"?
   —Wilde, "*Epistola*," in *The Complete Works of Oscar Wilde* (New York: HarperCollins, 1966), 933

7 Now the supposedly good brother shows that he, too, has a weakness. He can feel bitter envy. But we see no change in him. Although he was the good one, he is not in the kingdom.

8 This simple, moving story redirects our thinking. You do not live in harmony with the law of life by feeling special or in the right crowd. Following the rules will not get you into the kingdom. No, you have to live life fully, making your own mistakes, and then making a turn for the better and finding forgiveness. Notice the allusions to Jesus dying and coming back to life. The word for "dead" here is *nekron*, as in "necropolis." It can mean literally "dead" or metaphorically lifeless and lost—soul-dead. The story continues the theme of who belongs in the kingdom. In this case, it is not the good, well-behaved son but the one who made big mistakes and had a change of heart.

"The older brother got angry and wouldn't go in.[6] His father went outside and begged him. He told his father, 'All these years I have worked hard for you and never disobeyed you. But you never gave me even a young goat so I could party with my friends. But this son comes back after wasting your money on prostitutes, and you slaughter the well-fed calf for him.'[7]

"The father said, 'Son, you are always with me, and everything I have is yours. But we have to be happy and celebrate. Your brother was dead and has come back to life. He was lost and has been found.'"[8]

1   Once again, this is a story of someone who made a big mistake and did
something very wrong. Now what does he do? Wallow in his guilt? No, he
uses his imagination to make things better.

2   The contrast between worldly success and inner development is clear and
strong. In many cases, you will find it difficult to do both. One way to enter
the kingdom is to dedicate your energy to a visionary, utopian life.

Chapter 16

Jesus spoke again to his followers: "There was once a wealthy man who had an agent, who, people said, was squandering his possessions.[1] He called for the man and said, 'What is this that I hear about you? Give an account of your activities. You can't work for me any longer.'

"The agent thought, 'What am I going to do now? My boss is taking away my job. I'm not strong enough to dig and I'm ashamed to beg. I know what I'll do. When I lose my job, people will take me into their households.'

"He called on each of his master's debtors. He asked the first one, 'How much do you owe?' He said, 'Eight hundred gallons of olive oil.'

"The agent said, 'All right. Take your invoice and sit down quickly and make it four hundred.'

"Then he asked the second, 'What do you owe?'

"'A thousand bushels of wheat,' he said.

"'All right, take the invoice and make it eight hundred.'

"The master praised the dishonest agent because he had acted shrewdly. Worldly people are more shrewd in dealing with their own than with the children of light. I advise you to come to terms with worldly wealth, so that when it is gone you have a spiritual home.[2]

"A person who is trustworthy about little things will be trustworthy about big things as well. A person who is dishonest about little things will be dishonest about big things as well.

"If you haven't been trustworthy about worldly wealth, who could entrust you with real riches? If you haven't been trustworthy dealing with someone else's property, who will give you anything of your own?

3   This is not just a moralistic tirade against having money. The central point
    is, "You can't serve God and riches." Not at the same time. If your god is
    financial wealth, you cannot have an infinite God. But if you live a godly life,
    you can certainly give some attention to money. Just do not make it a god.

4   The Gospel of Luke is full of contrasts like this one between the rich man
    and poor Lazarus. Such a contrast helps us see the nature of the kingdom: Its
    values are usually the reverse of those we hold in ordinary life. Here poverty
    is an advantage.

5   This is another parable of reversed expectations. The wealthy man who
    enjoyed a successful life ends up in hell after death while the poor man fares
    well. This is how things are in the kingdom. What we normally judge as
    success is failure from the inverted and paradoxical values of the kingdom.
    John Dominic Crossan says, "Jesus was not interested in moral admonition
    on the dangers of riches." See Crossan, *In Parables: The Challenge of the Histori-
    cal Jesus* (Santa Rosa, CA: Polebridge Press, 1992), 66. Jesus is teaching how
    the kingdom works in ways opposed to the values of ordinary life today. We
    honor wealth and disdain poverty, but in the kingdom wealth is no indica-
    tion of success and happiness. Going without may teach you how to value
    what is truly important.

"A servant can't serve two masters. He'll hate one and love the other or be devoted to one and think little of the other. You can't serve God and riches."³

The Pharisees appreciated money and found all this absurd.

Jesus told them, "You justify your behavior with human values, but God knows your hearts. What people judge as excellent is idolatrous in the eyes of God.

"Until John, we preached the law and the prophets. Now the Great Teaching about the kingdom of God is being announced and everyone is demanding to be part of it. But it's easier for earth and sky to disappear than for a single flourish on a letter of the law to lose its authority.

"Anyone who divorces his spouse and marries another commits adultery. Anyone who marries someone who has divorced his or her spouse commits adultery.

"There was once a wealthy man who always dressed in purple and fine linen and lived happily in luxury every day. A poor man named Lazarus sat at his gate.⁴ He was covered with sores and craved to eat the crumbs that fell from the rich man's table. Even the dogs would come and lick his sores.

"The poor man died and angels came and carried him away to Abraham's lap. The rich man also died and was buried.

"Down in Hades he looked up in pain and saw Abraham far away and Lazarus in his lap. He shouted, 'Father Abraham, look kindly on me and send Lazarus to dip his finger in water and cool my tongue. This fire is torture.'⁵

6 The deep chasm is the difference between life in the kingdom and life outside of it. These two approaches to life are vastly different. One is based on
   love of self and neighbor and the other on self-aggrandizement.

"Abraham said, 'Child, remember how in life you enjoyed wonderful things and Lazarus had a bad time. Now he is finding comfort here and you're in distress. Besides, there's a deep chasm[6] between you and us. If you want to come over here, you'll find it impossible. No one can cross over from where you are to us.'

"The man said, 'Please, Father, send him to my father's house to warn my five brothers so they won't come to this dreadful place.'

"Abraham said, 'They could listen to Moses and the prophets.'

"'They won't. But if someone visits them from the dead, they'll have a change of heart.'

"Abraham answered, 'If they don't listen to Moses and the prophets, even if someone wakes up from death, they won't be persuaded.'"

1 It is bad enough to be outside the kingdom, living unconsciously and pursuing selfish goals. It is even worse to cause others to remain outside the kingdom. This is not about reward and punishment, but about the state of a person who lives in these ways. They are worse than lost. They may have worldly success but lack meaning and the happiness that comes from being in tune with the law of life.

2 The ways of the kingdom often seem odd, illogical, and unreasonable compared to ordinary ways that we are used to. Here our tolerance for our brother's mistakes must be vast. That is the way of the kingdom. Especially if he shows *metanoia*, a change of heart, we will forgive him no matter how bad he has been. Forgiveness is a special quality in the kingdom. It is the opposite of blame and any desire for revenge or vengeance.

3 Here we find two of the key internal achievements in the kingdom next to each other: forgiveness and trust. Both are difficult: Something in us does not want to forgive, and trust requires a letting go of control. To forgive, you must ignore all the reasoning that justifies vengeance and retaliation. Look at the international political climate. One government does something atrocious and another feels justified in retaliating. This is not the kingdom Jesus describes in his parables.

Chapter 17

Jesus said to his followers, "It can't be helped, obstacles will appear, but it's really unfortunate for the person responsible for them. He would be better off with a millstone around his neck and thrown into the sea than to cause just one innocent to stumble.[1]

"Be alert. If your brother makes a mistake, correct him. If he has a change of heart, forgive him. If he does something stupid to you seven times on one day and yet comes back and says, 'I'm sorry,' forgive him."[2]

The apostles said to the master, "Help us make our trust stronger."

The master said, "If you had trust the size of a mustard seed, you would say to a mulberry tree, 'Uproot yourself and plant yourself in the sea,' and it would obey you.[3] Say you have a servant who is plowing or tending sheep. When he returns from the field, will you say, 'Come right in, sit down, and eat'? Or will you say, 'Make me something to eat and get dressed and tend me while I eat and drink; later you can eat'?

"You don't thank the servant because he did things he was ordered to do, do you? The same with you. When you do everything you have been told to do, say, 'We are worthless servants. We've only done our duty.'"

4   The way Jesus heals requires the one healed to trust in the process. Joined to that trust is gratitude. In the story, we find a familiar reversal: Only the foreigner, the one you may not expect, makes an effort to express his thanks. This is how it is; those who should know better act badly. Those you might expect to be lacking in character show their mettle. We get it wrong when we admire displays of virtue. It is the unvirtuous who often act in exemplary ways.

5   "Reality has no need of other realities to bolster it. There are no divinities hidden in the trees, not any elusive thing-in-itself behind appearances, nor a mythological self that orders our actions. Life is truthful appearance."
    —Jorge Luis Borges, "The Nothingness of Personality," in *Jorge Luis Borges: Selected Non-Fictions*, edited by Eliot Weinberger (New York: Viking, 1999), 8

6   The Greek word *entos* can mean either "inside" or "among." I am using both meanings here, though I use the phrase "all around you." This is a key passage, because people often think of the kingdom as something in the future or somehow apart from this life and this world. As Henry David Thoreau writes, "I wish so to live as to derive my satisfactions & inspirations from the commonest events, so that what my senses hourly perceive, my daily walk, the conversation of my neighbors may inspire me, & I may dream of no heaven but that which lies about me."
    —Thoreau, in Ralph Waldo Emerson, *Emerson in His Journals*, edited by Joel Porte (Cambridge, MA: Belknap Press, 1982), 504

The following passage from Thich Nhat Hanh helps clarify this point: "A Zen follower asked, 'Where is the world of no-birth and no-death?' The master replied, 'It is right here in the world of birth and death.' . . . The world of nirvana is also the world of birth and death. . . . Abraham Heschel said that to live by the Torah, the Jewish law, is to live the life of eternity within time."
    —*Living Buddha, Living Christ* (New York: Riverhead Books, 1995), 149

7   Living the new life Jesus espouses requires your full attention and dedication. Do not be like Lot's wife in Genesis 19:26 and look back longingly on a former life. Give yourself to universal love, neighborliness, radical forgiveness, and unreasonable trust. Do not be concerned about trivial things that interfere with your engagement with the new law of love.

Jesus was on his way to Jerusalem and passing through Samaria and Galilee when, as he entered a town, ten lepers encountered him at a distance. They spoke up and said, "Jesus, Master, look kindly on us."

Seeing them, he said, "Go and let the priests see you." On their way their illness cleared up. One turned back, when he noticed that he'd been healed, and praised God loudly. Then he fell on his face at the feet of Jesus and thanked him. And he was a Samaritan!

Jesus said, "Weren't ten healed? Where are the other nine? Only this foreigner came back to honor God?" He said to the man, "Stand up and go. Your trust has made you better."[4]

The Pharisees asked Jesus when the kingdom of God was coming. He answered them, "The kingdom of God isn't arriving with obvious signs that can be seen.[5] People won't say, 'I see it. Here it is.' Or, 'There it is.' No, the kingdom of God is inside you and all around you."[6]

He said to his followers, "Soon you will wish it were one of the days when the son of man was here. But it won't be. People will shout, 'Here, no there.' Don't go anywhere. Don't chase after them. No, just like lightning flashing in one part of the sky illuminates other parts, so will the son of man be on his day. But first he has to suffer much and be rejected by his people. On that day, a person on the roof of his house shouldn't go down to get his possessions from the house. A person in a field shouldn't turn back. Remember Lot's wife.[7] Whoever tries to preserve his soul will lose it and whoever loses his soul will preserve it. I can tell you this, on that night two people will be in bed. One will be taken and the other left behind. Two women will be grinding flour in the same spot. One will be taken and the other left behind. Two men will be in a field. One will be taken and one left behind."

8 If we are not in the kingdom, not living out the law of love, we are like
corpses around whom the spirit of death circles, like vultures. To be in the
kingdom is to be alive. Many people appear to be soul-dead, at least in many
areas of life. Like robots, they go through life without the vivifying presence
of love and compassion.

They said to him, "Where, sir?"

He said, "Where the body is, there the vultures will gather."[8]

1   The persistence shown by the widow is a common theme in the Gospel of
    Luke. Apparently, it is an important virtue in the kingdom. Don't give up.
    Keep looking for what you need and want.

2   Following a utopian, love-based way of life requires endurance, faithfulness,
    and persistence. You have to trust that in the midst of injustice it is worth-
    while to remain loyal to your ideals, even if they go against the spirit of the
    times. Eventually, you may come to a point where you feel rewarded for
    your trust in this way of life.

3   Here we see another example of the upside-down logic of the kingdom. If
    you are proud, you will be humbled. If you practice genuine humility, you
    will discover that you are in a good place in life. The reward for good living
    is a deep peace and profound self-satisfaction.

Chapter 18

Then Jesus told his followers a parable to teach them to pray anytime and not give up. "There was once a judge in a town who didn't fear God or respect people. There was a widow in that town who kept coming to him, asking, 'Give me justice against my opponent.'

"For a while he refused. But then he thought, 'I don't fear God or care about people, but only because this widow keeps pestering me I'll see that she gets justice. Otherwise, she'll wear me out with her persistence.'"[1]

The master said, "Notice what this dishonest judge says. Won't God make justice available for his own special ones that implore him every night? Will he keep them waiting long? I say he'll give them justice quickly.[2] But when the son of man comes, will he find trust anywhere on the planet?"

To people who believed that they were good and considered others beneath them, he told this parable: "Two men went to the temple to pray, a Pharisee and a revenue clerk. The Pharisee prayed quietly, 'God, I'm just thankful that I'm not like other people—cheaters, criminals, adulterers, or like this tax man. I fast twice a week and pay tithes on everything I make.'

"The revenue officer, standing a good distance away, didn't want to raise his eyes to the sky but was beating his breast, 'God, be kind to me, a failure.'

"I would say that this man went home more virtuous than the other one. Anyone who puffs himself up will be humbled, and anyone who humbles himself will be given honor."[3]

4   The kingdom of the sky is for someone like a child. What does this mean? We know that if you feel privileged, virtuous, socially superior, or concerned with money you do not have much chance of being in the kingdom. We know that if you are a criminal, an offender, a sexual explorer, or a thief, you have special entrée to the kingdom. We might conclude that to be childlike here means not to possess the usual adult emotions of entitlement and self-control, but rather to be lacking in knowledge and self-control and therefore ready for the kingdom.

5   The word I translate as "timeless" is *aion*, which I understand as life unaffected by the limitations of time. This is "eternal life" in the sense of being outside the impact of time. We want to be in touch with our essential selves, a core of self that simply is and does not change.

6   Various writers offer rational explanations for this image of the camel and the needle. I prefer the plain and perhaps comic interpretation that the image is indeed about a camel and a needle. Simply, that is how difficult it is to be in the kingdom, where communal respect and concern are radically important, while being focused on money. If you make money your main concern, it will be almost impossible to live out the kingdom values and vision. But consider as well this esoteric reading of the image from the Indian philosopher Ananda K. Coomaraswamy: "The camel is the outer and existent person, So-and-So, as distinguished from the 'thread' or 'ray' of the spirit, which alone is his veritable essence and by which alone he can return through the 'eye' of the needle, which is also the solar 'eye,' to the source of his life."
    — Coomaraswamy, in Rama P. Coomaraswamy, ed., *The Door in the Sky: Coomaraswamy on Myth and Meaning* (Princeton, NJ: Princeton University Press, 1997), 51

7   It is difficult to imagine that there will be a day when human beings will live in peace and friendship and know how to really heal each other and enjoy each other's company. This ideal seems impossible, and yet Jesus calls on us to have faith in the ideal.

People brought toddlers to Jesus so he could hold them, but when his followers saw this they complained. Jesus said, "Let the children come to me. Don't get in their way, because the kingdom of God is for anyone like them. If you don't appreciate the kingdom of God as a child would, you can't get in."[4]

A leader asked him, "Good teacher, what do I have to do to merit a timeless life?"[5]

Jesus said, "Why do you call me good? Only God is good. Well, you know the commandments—do not commit adultery, do not murder, do not steal, do not perjure yourself, honor your mother and father."

He replied, "All this I've done since I was a child."

Jesus heard this and said, "There's still one thing missing: Sell everything you have and give it away to the poor. Then you'll have a treasure above. And come and follow me."

When the man heard this, he looked sad, for he was very wealthy.

Jesus looked at him and said, "It isn't easy for the wealthy to enter the kingdom of God. In fact, it's easier for a camel to pass through the eye of a needle than for a wealthy person to enter the kingdom of God."[6]

People listening to this asked, "Then who can be saved?"

Jesus said, "Some things humanly impossible are nevertheless possible with God."[7]

Peter said, "Yes, but we have left our home and joined up with you."

Jesus said, "I assure you, anyone who has left his home, wife, brothers, parents, or children for the kingdom of God will receive many times as much now and in the age that is approaching."

8 We could understand the "son of man" to mean any human being, or perhaps any human following the fate of Jesus. We will be persecuted, especially for our values, but we will rise up again. We need the trust and hope that, having been defeated, we can appear again with our ideals intact.

9 Is this healing of the blind man an example of Jesus caring for the unfortunate or showing that he has special powers of healing? Or could it be that to be in the kingdom we all need to be cured of our blindness, our failure to see how life needs to be lived, for us all to be happy and fulfilled? Again, notice the disparity between the trusting man and the derisive crowd.

Then he took the twelve aside and told them, "We're going to Jerusalem now and everything the prophets wrote about the son of man will take place. He'll be handed over to non-Jews and will be mocked and mistreated and spat upon. After they torture him, they'll kill him, but on the third day he will reappear."[8]

The followers didn't understand any of this. His message escaped them. They couldn't comprehend it.

As Jesus was drawing near to Jericho, a blind man was sitting on the road begging. Hearing the crowd go by, he asked who was passing. People told him that it was Jesus of Nazareth. So he called out, "Jesus, son of David, look kindly on me."

People leading the entourage scolded him and told him to be quiet, but he only shouted more loudly, "Son of David, be merciful to me."

Jesus stopped and told them to bring the man to him. When the man got close enough, Jesus asked him, "What do you want me to do for you?"

He said, "Sir, I'd like to have my sight back."

Jesus said, "Then have your sight back. Your trust has made you better."

Instantly the man regained his sight and joined up with Jesus, giving honor to God. When the people saw all this, they, too, gave honor to God.[9]

1 Again we have a man who cannot "see." In this case, he is too small. You could imagine that he is not only small in stature, as in the story, but also small in vision. Jesus's teaching is based on a great vision for humanity, and it is important for small-minded people to climb a tree and get a better view of what he is talking about.

2 A charming story about Jesus's typical choice of an improbable and unlikely follower. Author Lynda Sexson quotes this dream text: "Once Jesus appeared in a dream to comfort me. I thought it was lovely of him to come, considering that I didn't believe in him."
   —Sexson, *Ordinarily Sacred* (New York: Crossroad, 1982), 101

3 The gospel challenge is not as sweet and sentimental as it is sometimes presented. It requires both ingenuity and personal strength.

Chapter 19

He entered Jericho and was passing through the city. There was a man there named Zaccheus, a wealthy head revenue officer. Zaccheus was small and couldn't see through the crowd to get a glimpse of Jesus. So he ran ahead and climbed up a sycamore tree to see him.[1] Jesus was just about to pass by. When Jesus did indeed reach that spot, he looked up and said, "Zaccheus, quick, come down from there. I'm going to stay at your house today." Zaccheus quickly came down and was happy to welcome Jesus.

People watched all this unfold and grumbled, "He's off to be the guest of a man who lives a questionable life."

Zaccheus stopped and said to the master, "Sir, half of what I own I'll give to the poor, and if I've cheated anyone, I'll give back four times what I owe them."

Jesus said, "Today deliverance has come to this house, because this man is also a son of Abraham. The son of man has come to search out and rescue whoever is lost."[2]

While people were listening to his words, Jesus went on to tell a parable. Since he was near Jerusalem they assumed that the kingdom of God was going to appear immediately.

He said, "An important man went to a far-off country to accept a royal office and then return. He called for ten of his servants and gave them about four thousand dollars. He told them, 'Do something with this money until I return.'

"But his people didn't like him and they sent a representative after him, saying, 'We don't want this man to have authority over us.'

"When he returned, after receiving the state benefits, he instructed that the servants to whom he had given money be called in. He wanted to know what they had accomplished with it.[3]

4   Fear is one of those things that can get in the way. We must find the courage
    to be clever and strong enough to dare to live in the kingdom.

5   This is one of several confounding statements in this Gospel. Of course, it
    upends conventional wisdom and logic. Ordinarily, you might think that the
    "haves" will lose something and the "have nots" will gain something. Not so
    here. Perhaps it means that in the special logic and values of the kingdom,
    you come into this new world with certain ideas and values, such as a child-
    like openness and an interest in sharing the wealth. As you go further into
    the reality of the kingdom, this precious vitality and sense of community
    increases. If you approach it without these ideas, what little you have may
    be lost. Certainly if you expect the kingdom to give you the earthly and ego
    satisfactions that you lack, you will be disappointed.

"The first one showed up and said, 'Master, your four thousand dollars has made ten times as much.'

"He said to the servant, 'Excellent. Good job. Because you have been trustworthy with very little, you'll have authority over ten cities.'

"The second came forward and said, 'Your four thousand has made twenty.'

"The master said, 'You will govern five cities.'

"Still another came, 'Master, here is your four thousand dollars. I kept it hidden in a rag. I was afraid of you.[4] You're a demanding person. You pick things up that you haven't put down and harvest things you never planted.'

"The master said, 'I'll judge you by your words, you worthless employee. If you thought I was a demanding person who picks up what he doesn't put down and harvests what he doesn't plant, why didn't you put the money in the bank? When I returned I could have taken it out with interest.'

"Then he said to those standing around, 'Take the four thousand away from him and give it to the one who has ten.'

"'But he already has ten thousand,' they said.

"'Yes, but more will be given to those who already have something. Those who don't have anything will lose what they have.'[5] Now, as to those enemies of mine who didn't want my authority, bring them here and kill them in front of me."

After this story, Jesus and his followers kept on going toward Jerusalem. They got to Bethphage and Bethany, near the Mount of Olives, and he sent out two followers, telling them, "Go to the village ahead of us. When you first enter you'll find a young donkey tied up. No one has ever sat on her. Untie her and bring her here. If anyone asks you why you're letting her free, say that the master needs her."

6 "The mythical motif of 'riding on a donkey' is often taken as a sign of humility. It also has a more mystical meaning, however. To the ancients the donkey typified lust, cruelty, and wickedness. It symbolically represented the
   lower 'animal' self, which must be overcome and subdued by an initiate of
   the Mysteries."
      —Timothy Freke and Peter Gandy, *The Jesus Mysteries: Was the "Original Jesus" a
      Pagan God?* (New York: Three Rivers Press, 1999), 44

7 "They saw lives [those of Jesus's followers] that had been transformed—men
   and women who were ordinary in every way except for the fact that they
   seemed to have found the secret of living. They evinced a tranquility, simplicity and cheerfulness that their hearers had nowhere else encountered. . . .
   In the midst of their trials, they had laid hold of an inner peace that found
   expression in a joy that seemed exuberant. Perhaps *radiant* would be a better
   word."
      —Huston Smith, *The World's Religions* (New York: HarperCollins, 1991), 331–
      332

8 People who sell salvation are all around us, and sometimes they do their
   business quietly and with subtlety. They turn spirituality into a commodity.
   Many are gullible and give their souls away. No wonder Jesus shows unchar-
   acteristic anger in the temple.

So they went off and found things just as he had said they
would. They were just untying the donkey when its owners said
to them, "Why are you taking her?"

"The master needs her," they said.

They brought the donkey[6] to Jesus and put their coats on
her and then sat Jesus on her.

As he went along, people spread their garments on the road,
and when he was drawing near the lower part of the Mount
of Olives, the whole crowd of followers praised God with joy
and a loud voice for all the wonders they had witnessed. They
shouted, "Blessed is the king who comes in the name of the
Lord. May peace be in the heavens and honor in the cosmos."[7]

Some of the Pharisees in the crowd said, "Teacher, restrain
your followers."

Jesus said, "If they are silent, the very stones will shout."

He came to Jerusalem and looked over the city and wept. "If
only you knew now what would bring you peace. But you can't
see it now. The day will come when your enemies will build
a barricade around you and block you in from every angle.
They'll raze you to the ground, your children with you, and
they won't leave one stone on top of another, all because you
didn't understand your fate."

Jesus entered the temple and drove out the ones who were
selling things, saying, "It was written, 'My house will be a house
of prayer, and yet you have turned it into a den of thieves.'"[8]

He taught in the temple daily, and the chief priests and
experts in the law and other leaders tried to get rid of him. But
they couldn't find a way, since the people all listened attentively
to every word he spoke.

1   This is a good question. Jesus does speak with a strong sense of authority. Where does he get this? From his religion? Apparently not. His adversaries in this passage have that kind of authority. Does it come from his sense of mission and vision? What does this say about Jesus as an exemplar? Should we look for an inner authority, a sense of mission based on our vision? How do you speak with authority about spiritual matters? Do you get authority partly from a tradition and partly from your own inspiration? Should you cede authority to particular leaders or a church, or is that going against the Jesus way here?

2   One essential ingredient for a rich spiritual life is usually ignored: intelligence. But Jesus always uses his wits. He is not an easy mark for spiritual charlatans, and neither should we be.

Chapter 20

One day Jesus was teaching in the temple, presenting the gospel message, when the chief priests, experts in the law, and elders approached him. They said, "Tell us what authority you have for doing these things. Who gave you this authority?"[1]

Jesus answered, "Let me ask you a question. Was John's baptizing heavenly or earthly?"

They discussed the question, thinking, "If we say, 'heavenly,' then he'll say, 'Why don't you trust me?' But if we say, 'earthly,' the people will all stone us to death. They're certain that John was a prophet." So they answered that they didn't know where it came from.

Jesus said, "I won't tell you where I get my authority to do these things, either."[2]

Then Jesus told the people this parable: "A man planted a vineyard and rented it to gardeners. Then he went on a long trip. At harvest time he sent a servant to the gardeners to get some of the produce from the vineyard. But the gardeners beat up the servant and sent him off empty-handed.

"The man sent another servant. They beat him up, too, and treated him roughly and sent him off empty-handed.

"He sent a third servant, and this one they hurt and threw out.

"The owner thought, 'What should I do? I know, I'll send my dear son. Maybe they'll show him respect.' But when the gardeners saw him, they plotted. 'This one's the heir. Let's kill him and get the inheritance.' So they dragged him off the vineyard and killed him.

"So what will the owner of the vineyard do to them? He'll kill the gardeners and give the vineyard to someone else."

3   This vineyard is our hope for a better life. Let's hope that we, humanity, do
    not kill the owner and lose our chance for a meaningful life. Let's hope that
    we are not condemned to our folly and insanity.

4   Here we have yet another version of the great reversal at the heart of the
    Gospels: Those the world has rejected will become the cornerstone of the
    new way, the kingdom. Those who trusted in such things as virtue, self-
    denial, mere churchgoing, and the appearance of godliness will be wiped out.

5   We live in two worlds, the ordinary life of daily commerce and the utopian
    realm of our ideals. We must give something to both. Those who follow the
    regular way of life do not understand us utopians and are suspicious of us.

6   You do not have to take this only literally. They deny that humanity can res-
    urrect into a more perfect life where love is the rule and absolute forgiveness
    the sign of the kingdom.

When the people heard the story, they said, "Let's hope this never comes to pass."[3]

But Jesus looked at them and said, "What about the saying, 'The stone that the builders rejected became the cornerstone'? Anyone who falls on that stone will be smashed to bits, but anyone it falls on will blow away like dust."[4]

The experts in the law and the chief priests wanted to grab him at that moment, but they were afraid of the people. They knew that the parable was directed at them. They watched him closely and sent spies, who pretended to be among the enlightened, so that they could catch him saying something that would allow them to hand him over to the rule and authority of the governor.

They asked him, "Teacher, we understand that you speak and teach properly. You are not biased but teach the way of God honestly. But tell us, is it legal for us to pay taxes to Caesar?"

He saw their trickery and said, "Hand me a denarius. Whose picture and words are on it?"

They said, "Caesar's."

He said, "Then render to Caesar the things that are Caesar's and to God the things that are God's."[5]

They had failed to snare him into saying something dangerous in the people's presence. They were surprised by his response and at a loss for words.

One of the Sadducees (they deny resurrection)[6] asked him, "Teacher, Moses wrote that if a man dies, has a wife, and is childless, his brother should marry the wife and raise his brother's children. Well, one time there were seven brothers. The first was married and died childless. The second one, as well. The third married her, too. The same with all seven, who died, leaving no children. Finally, the woman died, too. In the resurrection, whose wife will she be? All seven married her."

7   This is a serious challenge. It is true that in ordinary life people get married and often suffer the challenge of monogamy. Could it be that, in the kingdom, marriage changes radically or becomes something else entirely?

8   Psalm 110:1.

9   This is a widespread problem in spiritual circles. People who profess high moral standards often act in the opposite way. Jesus frequently advises against pretending to be holier than everyone else.

Jesus said, "In this life sons marry and are given in marriage, but those who have attained resurrection don't marry.[7] Nor are they given in marriage. They no longer die, because they're like angels, sons of God, sons of the resurrection.

"In the passage about the burning bush, where he calls on the God of Abraham, Isaac, and Jacob, Moses taught that the dead resurrect. He is not the God of the dead but of the living. To him everyone is alive."

Some experts in the law responded, "Teacher, you have spoken well." They didn't dare ask him any more questions.

Jesus said, "Why would they say that Christos is David's son?

"In the Book of Psalms, David says,

'The Lord said to my Lord
sit on my right side
until I make your enemies
a cushion for my feet.'[8]

"See, David calls him 'Lord,' so how could he be his son?"

While the people were listening to this, he said to his followers: "Watch out for the experts in the law. They like to walk around in long robes and be greeted with respect in the marketplace and enjoy seats of privilege in the synagogues and at banquets. But they take over widows' houses and make a show of saying long prayers. They will suffer stiff punishment."[9]

1   This is yet another kind of reversal. The person with little to show offers an immense gift that may amount to nothing in someone else's circumstances.

2   You do not have to take these apocalyptic descriptions literally. In some ways we may well suffer social upheaval and disaster because we do not follow the universal teachings that love and respect are the basis of all relationships.

3   It is essential to remain mindful of the teachings about utopian life in the kingdom. You do not have to defend yourself. You can just let your vision of life guide you and inform your words. There is great power in the vision of a new kind of humanity.

Chapter 21

Jesus looked around and saw the wealthy putting their gifts into the temple treasury. He also watched a poor widow drop in two small copper coins. "The truth is," he said, "that the widow has contributed more than the others. The others drew on their great wealth for their gift, but she in her poverty gave away everything she had to live on."[1]

Some of the followers pointed out that the temple was adorned with beautiful stonework and with articles given for God. Jesus said, "Well, you see all this now, but the time will come when one stone won't be left standing on another. Every single one will be demolished."

They said, "Teacher, when will this happen and how will we know that it's about to happen? Will there be signs?"

"Take care that you're not deceived," he said. "Many will appear using my name. They'll say, 'I'm the one.' 'The time has come.' But don't follow them. When you hear of wars and rebellions, don't be afraid. These things will necessarily take place, but it doesn't mean that the end time has arrived.

"Nation will rise up against nation and kingdom against kingdom. There will be earthquakes and famines and plagues. There will be disasters and other signs from the sky. Before these things happen people will grab hold of you and persecute you, delivering you over to those in the synagogues and prisons, bringing you up before kings and rulers, all for my sake. You will have an opportunity to bear witness.[2]

"Decide now not to prepare to defend yourselves. I will give you both the wisdom and the words that your opponents won't be able to counter or refute.[3] Parents, brothers, relatives, and friends will betray you and, in some cases, put you to death. Because of my name, almost everyone will hate you.

4   Not only has the kingdom not come to pass, but the world has totally suc-
    cumbed to its insane values and goals. Jesus offers an alternative that would
    save humankind from disaster, but the world has not paid attention. The
    apocalyptic disaster is coming to pass with our planet consumed with con-
    flict and violence. This is the end time. We are in it. It is a question of
    whether we can recover our senses and avoid total calamity.

5   "The domain of God is the result of the deconstruction of the old world
    and the fabrication of the new. . . . The alternative reality is the unreachable
    destination of a perpetual journey. Like Moses, we are not permitted to cross
    over to the promised land. . . . If we think we have arrived, we have only
    fallen back into the grip of the old. That is the power of 'Satan.' Satan stands
    for stagnation."
        —Robert W. Funk, *A Credible Jesus: Fragments of a Vision* (Santa Rosa, CA:
        Polebridge Press, 2002), 160–161

6   There are a few signs of the fig tree blossoming today in society—women's
    rights, opposition to racism, awareness of spiritual aspects of medicine—but
    the tree is not healthy. It is still possible to tend the fig tree in personal life.

7   We must read the signs of unconsciousness and self-interest. Then we can
    remember the Great Teaching and return to the principles of love and
    respect.

"But not a hair of your head will perish. By your faithfulness you will gain your souls.

"When you see Jerusalem surrounded by armies, then you can assume that her destruction is close at hand. Then those in Judea will have to flee to the mountains, those in the city will have to leave, and those in the country must avoid the city.

"These will be days of vengeance. I pity pregnant women and nursing mothers at that time. The distress and rage will be unimaginable. People will fall to the sword and be led captive in all countries. Foreigners will trample on Jerusalem and will be victorious.[4]

"The sun, moon, and stars will signal the end time, and on the earth international strife and concern about the vehemence of the seas and gales will be part of it.[5]

"The delicate workings of the sky will go haywire, and people will swoon from fear and worry about what is happening in the world. Then they'll see the son of man arriving in a mist with power and magnificent splendor.

"When all this begins to happen, stand up and raise your heads. Your fulfillment is near."

He told them a parable: "Look how a fig tree, or any tree, puts out leaves and thereby signals that summer is approaching. Similarly, when you see all these things happening that I have mentioned, realize that the kingdom of God is near. I assure you, this generation will not pass on until all these things take place. The earth and the sky may pass, but not my words.[6]

"Be careful to not let the depression of your hearts lead you to engage in lives of dissipation and drunkenness. Don't worry. That day won't come on you suddenly like a trap.[7] It will come for everyone living on the face of the earth.

"Still, always be alert. Pray that you have the strength to get away from all these things that are going to happen and to stand strong for the son of man."

8 Jesus models a way of life that is both active and contemplative: teaching in public and praying at night.

During the day he would teach in the temple and in the evening he would go and spend the night on the Mount of Olives.[8] People would get up early to go to the temple to hear him.

1   "John turned Jesus into a redeeming Passover Lamb. For the Christos of John
    expired on the cross in the afternoon of the day *preceding* the Passover, and
    thus his death exactly coincided with the slaughtering of the Passover lambs
    in the courtyard of the Temple of Jerusalem."
        —Geza Vermes, *The Changing Faces of Jesus* (New York: Penguin, 2000), 40

2   This detail about getting ready for the Passover meal seems unnecessary
    and could be implied. That it is spelled out indicates Jesus's engagement
    in his community and among his friends, and his attention to the ordinary
    requirements of daily life. It is also a sign of his Epicureanism, his love for his
    friends and celebrating with them. This love of ordinary life is also part of
    the kingdom.

3   Not that the kingdom itself has fully arrived, but that preparations are com-
    ing to an end.

4   Bread became part of a ritual, but here it is also a profound metaphor for
    Jesus—his example, teaching, stories, and poetic metaphors in general. In all
    these things he is nourishment for the soul and spirit.

Chapter 22

The Festival of the Unleavened Bread, Passover, was drawing near. The chief priests were trying to figure out how to put Jesus to death. They were still afraid of the people. Then Satan entered into Judas Iscariot, one of the twelve, and he went to the chief priests and officials and discussed how he could turn him in to them. They were satisfied and offered him some money. He decided to go along and would seek an opportunity to betray Jesus when he was away from a crowd.

The first day of the festival arrived, when the Passover lamb would be sacrificed. Jesus sent Peter and John. "Go and get ready for the Passover so we can all eat together."[1]

"Where would you like us to prepare it?" they asked.

He told them, "When you enter the city, a man carrying a jug of water will greet you. Follow him into the house he enters. Tell the owner, 'The teacher told us to ask you a question: "Where is a suitable room where I can eat the Passover with my followers?"' He will show you a large, furnished upper room. Prepare the meal there."

They went and found everything exactly as he told them and they got everything ready for the Passover.[2]

When the time arrived, Jesus sat at the table with his apostles and said, "I have dearly wanted to eat this Passover with you before my ordeal. I can say to you now that I will not eat it again until the kingdom of God is complete."[3]

He took a cup and gave thanks and said, "Take this and share it among yourselves. I won't drink wine again until the kingdom of God arrives." He took bread and gave thanks and broke it and gave it to them and said, "This is my body[4] given up for you. Do this yourselves as a way of remembering me."

5 Jesus's followers do not seem to have grown much. They are still vying for top position and claiming moral superiority. One could imagine that they would become enlightened and would have matured. Instead, they retain their ignorance and childish ways, just as many do who have heard the teaching about the kingdom. In biblical scholar George Nickelsburg's words, "Luke sees Satan lurking about, first in the temptation, then in Judas and then with Peter, and with the warning in Gethsemane about temptation."

6 As usual, Jesus looks for metaphors and signs. Here, the rooster. The rooster crows to let us know it is morning, and here it crows to let us know when we have betrayed the son of God.

"Peter's attribute, the cock, gives him a solar character. After Christ's ascension he becomes the visible representative of God and replaces the chief deity of the Roman imperium, the *Sol invictus* [Sun unconquered]."

—C. G. Jung, "Symbols of Transformation," translated by R. F. C Hull, in *Collected Works of C. G. Jung*, vol. 5 (Princeton, NJ: Princeton University Press, 1967), sec. 289

Similarly, after the meal he took the cup and said, "This cup, emptied out for all of you, is the new way of life embodied in my blood. But, see, the hand of my betrayer is next to mine on this table. Yes, the son of man is going to his fate. But pity the man who betrays him."

They huddled and considered which of them might do such a thing. And they argued about who among them was the greatest.[5]

Jesus said, "Kings of secular nations lord it over their people, and they themselves have their authorities, 'allies' they call them. But this isn't your style. Whoever is greatest among you must act like a child and the leader like a servant. After all, who is greater—the person who sits at the table or the one who serves?

"Isn't it the person who sits at the table? And yet with you I play the role of servant. You have stood by me in my struggles, and just as my father has given me this 'kingdom,' I give you the opportunity to eat and drink at my kingdom table. You'll sit on seats judging the twelve tribes of Israel.

"Simon, Simon. You see, Satan has asked to be allowed to sift you like wheat, but I have prayed for you that your trust won't fail you. When you have recovered, support your brothers."

Peter said, "Sir, I'm prepared to go to prison and to be put to death with you."

Jesus said, "Peter, I'm telling you, the rooster won't crow today until you have denied three times that you know me."[6]

He addressed them all: "When I sent you out without a backpack or a money clip or even sandals, you didn't lack anything, did you?"

"No," they said, "nothing."

"But now, if you have a wallet, take it. Or a backpack. If you don't have a sword, sell your coat and buy one. You see, I have to fulfill what was written about me: 'He was one of the criminals.' I have to fulfill whatever was written about me."

7   There is a warrior quality in all spiritual traditions, and we see it here with
    Jesus. But it refers to force of character, rather than literal violence.

8   Jesus can live with the complexity of wanting his problem to go away so he
    will not suffer and yet also wanting to live out the fate determined by des-
    tiny or his Father's plan.

9   There is considerable irony in this kiss, since Jesus had been affectionate
    with the twelve men who were his closest companions and students. It is the
    inverse of *agape,* the love word that appears so many times in the Gospels.

They said, "Sir, here, we have two swords."

He said, "That's enough."[7]

He went outside and walked to the Mount of Olives as usual and his followers followed him. When he arrived there, he said, "Pray that you don't give in to temptations." He went about a stone's throw from them and knelt and prayed. "Father, if you are willing, take this cup from me, but what I want is not important. May your wishes be fulfilled."[8]

An angel from the sky appeared to him, giving him strength. But he was in pain and prayed earnestly. His sweat was like drops of blood dripping on the ground. He got up from praying and went over to his followers and found them sleeping. They were sad. He said, "Why are you sleeping? Get up and pray that you won't be tempted."

As he was speaking, a crowd arrived and Judas, one of the twelve, was leading them. He came forward and kissed Jesus.[9] Jesus said, "Judas, are you betraying the son of man with a kiss?"

His companions saw what was about to happen and said, "Sir, will we use our swords?" In fact, one of them struck the high priest's slave and sliced off his right ear. Jesus said, "No. No more of this." He touched the ear and healed it. Then Jesus spoke to the chief priests and officials of the temple and an elder who had come to oppose him. "Have you come out with swords and clubs as though I were a thief? When I was with you day after day in the temple, you didn't grab me. But apparently you like this late hour and the advantage of darkness."

They arrested him and led him away to the house of the high priest. Peter followed at a distance. They lit a fire in the middle of the courtyard and sat down. Peter sat among them, and a servant girl, staring at him as he sat in the light of the fire, said, "This fellow was with him." He denied it. "Girl, I don't even know him."

Later, another person saw Peter and said, "You're one of them, too."

10 Weeping bitterly, Peter is not just regretful. His remorse initiates him to a deeper level of awareness and understanding. Psychologist James Hillman writes, "The broken promise is a breakthrough of life in the world of Logos security, where the order of everything can be depended upon and the past guarantees the future. The broken promise or broken trust is at the same time a breakthrough onto another level of consciousness."
> —Hillman, "Betrayal," in *Loose Ends: Primary Papers in Archetypal Psychology* (Dallas: Spring Publications, 1975), 67

11 At this point Jesus is deep in the transition from his personal embodiment of the law of love to his presence in a "body" of teaching and a community of followers. The soldiers and judges can condemn and torture him now, but later the power of his teaching and vision will have great influence.

12 We are all sons and daughters of God when we honor the laws of life and work toward the self-realization of all beings.

Peter said, "I am not."

An hour later, yet another man insisted, "I'm sure of it. This man was with Jesus. He's Galilean as well."

Peter said, "I don't know what you're talking about."

Instantly, as he was speaking, a rooster crowed.

The master turned around and looked at Peter, who remembered what the master had told him: "Before a rooster crows today, you will deny me three times."

Peter left and wept bitterly.[10]

The men keeping Jesus in custody mocked him and beat him up. They put a blindfold on him and shouted, "Prophesy. Who hit you?"

They hurled many words of mockery at him.

At daylight, the council of elders assembled, chief priests and experts in the law, and led him to their council chamber. "If you are Christos, tell us," they said.

But he said, "You won't believe what I tell you, and if I ask you something, you won't answer me. But, from this moment forward, the son of man will sit at the right hand of God in power."[11]

They all asked him, "Are you the son of God?"[12]

"Yes, I am," he said.

"We don't need any more evidence. We've heard enough from his own mouth."

1   "The discovery of Q also cautions us about the traditional view that Christianity emerged as a reformation of the religion of Judaism. Even the appeal
to the epic of Israel was an ad hoc strategy that was not integral to the primary motivations of the Jesus movement. Other ideological resources were
as much in play, including popular forms of Hellenistic philosophy and the
mythology of wisdom. The attraction of the new community was . . . in the
enhancement of human values experienced in the process of social forma-
tion itself."
   —Burton L. Mack, *The Lost Gospel: The Book of Q and Christian Origins* (San
   Francisco: HarperSanFrancisco, 1993), 213

2   You would think that, once Pilate finds Jesus officially not guilty, that would
be the end of it. But human beings are moved by quiet, background themes
and narratives that are barely visible. These are often more persuasive than
logic.

Chapter 23

They all got up together and presented him to Pilate. They accused him. "We have found this man leading our nation astray. He argues against paying taxes to Caesar. He says that he himself is Christos and a king."

Pilate asked him, "Are you the king of the Jews?"

Jesus answered, "You are the one who is saying this."[1]

Pilate spoke to the chief priests and the people. "I find this man not guilty."[2]

But they pressed the matter. "He riles the people, speaking in public all over Judea, from Galilee to here."

Pilate latched on to this and said, "Is he a Galilean?"

He learned that Jesus belonged to Herod's jurisdiction and sent him to Herod, who was in Jerusalem at that time.

Herod was happy to see Jesus. In fact, he had wanted to see him for a long time. He had heard about him and was hoping to see some kind of demonstration from him. He questioned him at considerable length. But Jesus didn't say a word.

The chief priests and experts in the law were present, and they accused him vehemently.

Herod and his soldiers belittled him and mocked him and dressed him in a splendid robe and sent him off to Pilate. Herod and Pilate became friends that day. Before then they had been opponents. Pilate summoned the chief priests, the leaders, and the people, and said to them, "You brought this man to me because you say he incites people to rebel. But I've examined him in your presence and have found him not guilty of these charges. Herod, too, found him not guilty and sent him back here. He's done nothing that merits the death penalty. So, I'll beat him and let him go."

3 The story of Barabbas is a fascinating one. Researchers have found no evidence of the practice of releasing prisoners, except for a rather remote Greek example. The name Barabbas means "son of the father," remarkably similar to Jesus, and, in fact, in some texts of the Gospels he is called Jesus Barabbas. This leads some experts to think that this is a story that splits Jesus into two parts, Christos and the revolutionary. Perhaps the story shows that Jesus is both the radical critic and the anointed savior.

4 Crowds do not think. They get swept away by passion. Choosing to punish a real criminal instead of Jesus, the teacher of loving friendship, is too logical. The passion is for Jesus to be killed for being a serious threat, not to social peace but to emotional comfort.

5 Resisting Jesus's vision for humanity is equivalent to choosing a violent and meaningless way of life. Those who go this way inflict the punishment of self-annihilation on themselves.

6 "Christos crucified is the 'true Orpheus,' who carried home mankind as his bride from the depths of dark Hades—the *Orpheus Bakkikos*, as he is called in a famous early Christian representation of the crucifixion."
   —Hugo Rahner, "The Christian Mystery and the Pagan Mysteries," in *The Mysteries: Papers from the Eranos Yearbooks* (Princeton, NJ: Princeton University Press, 1955), 379

7 Details of the execution, like this one, show how sacrilegious the rejection of Jesus is. An odd anger can arise when a person is challenged to live a better life. People often prefer to be lost and then left unbothered in their desolation.

It was a time of festival, and he was required to pardon a prisoner. But the people shouted, "Kill this one. Free Barabbas." Barabbas was in prison for inciting an insurrection in the city and for murder.³

Pilate wanted to free Jesus, so he spoke to them once again. But the people kept shouting, "Crucify, crucify him."

For a third time, Pilate said, "Why? What crime has he committed? I find nothing that would demand the death penalty. So I'll just torture him and let him go."

But they wouldn't stop. They shouted out loudly, asking that Jesus be crucified.⁴ Eventually, their shouts prevailed. Pilate pronounced the sentence they wanted and pardoned the man they asked for and who had been in prison for insurrection and murder. Pilate delivered Jesus to them to do what they wanted.

They led him off and grabbed a man name Simon, from Cyrene, who had come in from the countryside, and put the cross on him to carry behind Jesus. A large crowd, including women, followed him, wailing and crying. Jesus turned toward them and said, "Daughters of Jerusalem, don't weep for me but for yourselves and your children. The day will come when people will say, 'Wombs that never bore children and breasts that never nursed are blessed.' To the mountains they will say, 'Crash down on us' and to the hills, 'Cover us over.'⁵

"If people do such things when the grass is green, just imagine what they'll do when it's brown."

They also dragged two criminals to be put to death with Jesus. They finally arrived at the place called Skull and crucified him there, along with the criminals, one on his right and one on his left. Jesus said, "Father, forgive them. They don't know what they're doing."⁶

They split his clothes among them by throwing dice.⁷

8   Here we have the culmination of Jesus's appreciation of the criminal. The thief acknowledges his life of crime and asks forgiveness. He is the perfect candidate for the kingdom. He has no sense of virtue or entitlement. He asks for consideration as a pure grace and favor. He does not deserve the kingdom, but he asks for it.

9   It was truly the darkest of days, because it marked the end, at least for the moment, of any hope that humanity would find itself and come into the life-giving rays of the sun. Jesus has been called the Sun of God.

10   The centurion, a foreigner and an occupier, understands. This is an old and familiar theme. Those who are not part of the fold will see what those in the inner circle do not see. The kingdom is not for the obvious believers but for those who have the gift of deep insight.

11   The women who supported Jesus during the days of his wanderings, when he presented the idea of a kingdom of the sky, utopian and love-based, are present here. But there is no mention of the men who so often asked to be right there with Jesus in a place of honor and privilege.

People were standing by, looking on. The leaders scorned him and said, "He saved other people. If this is Christos, the anointed of God, his special one, let's see him save himself." Soldiers, too, made fun of him, giving him sour wine and saying, "If you're the king of the Jews, save yourself."

They put a sign above him, THE KING OF THE JEWS.

One of the criminals hanging there shouted abuse at him, "You're Christos? Then save yourself and us, too." But the other one countered with a rebuke, "Don't you fear God? You are also condemned to die. But we deserve our suffering. We're getting our due because of our actions. This man has done nothing wrong. Jesus, remember me when you get to your kingdom."

Jesus said, "I assure you, this very day you will be with me in Paradise."[8]

It was the sixth hour. Darkness had fallen over the entire area until the ninth hour. The sun was shaded.[9] The temple veil split in two. Jesus cried out loudly, "Father, I give my spirit over into your hands." And then he breathed his last breath.

A centurion saw all of this and praised God, "This man was definitely innocent."[10]

Crowds gathered for this spectacle and watched everything that happened. They went back home beating their chests. His friends and the women from Galilee[11] who supported him stood off at a distance, watching. A man named Joseph, from the Jewish town of Arimathea, a member of the council and a good and honest man who had not agreed to the plot against Jesus, who was also waiting for the arrival of God's kingdom, went to Pilate and asked for Jesus's body. He took it down and wrapped it in a linen cloth and laid him in a tomb cut into rock, a fresh unoccupied tomb.

On Preparation Day, at the beginning of the Sabbath, women who had come with him from Galilee saw the tomb and noticed how he was laid out. They came back with spices and perfumes. On the Sabbath they observed the law and rested.

1   The Greek word for "risen" here is *egerthe*, the same word we encounter sev-
    eral times as "get up," as when Jesus healed someone and that person "got up"
    and walked. One of the chief movements in Jesus's teaching is "getting up"
    out of sleep or sickness. We all must get up—resurrect, if you will. We must
    stand up and live as individuals in a sleeping world.

2   The way of the world: The men, longtime students of Jesus, do not believe
    the women. They must go and see for themselves. Peter especially seems to
    have a particular problem with Mary of Magdala. Apparently, he does not
    like her strength and intelligence. In the Gospel of Mary Peter says with
    some bitterness: "Did he [the Savior] speak with a woman in private with-
    out our knowing about it? Are we to turn around and listen to her? Did he
    choose her over us?"
        —Karen L. King, *The Gospel of Mary of Magdala: Jesus and the First Woman Apostle*
        (Santa Rosa, CA: Polebridge Press, 2013), 17

3   *Shall I tell you again the new word,*
    the new word of the unborn day?
    It is Resurrection.
    The resurrection of the flesh.

    For our flesh is dead
    only egoistically we assert ourselves.

    And the new word means nothing to us,
    it is such an old word,
    till we admit how dead we are,
    till we actually feel as blank as we really are.
        —D. H. Lawrence, "The New Word" (1929)

4   The simple Greek word *mona*, "nothing more," tells a huge tale. Jesus is not
    there. The tomb is empty. He is no longer present in the flesh but now resur-
    rected in his teachings and among his followers, as he said he would be.

Chapter 24

Early in the morning on the first day of the week, the women went to the tomb with the spices they had prepared but discovered that the stone had been rolled away from the tomb. When they entered, they didn't see the body of the master. They were confused about this, but then two men dressed in shimmering clothes stood there right next to them. The women were frightened and bowed toward the ground, but the men said to them, "Why are you looking for someone alive here among the dead? He isn't here. He has risen.[1] Do you remember what he said in Galilee? He said that the son of man would be given over into the hands of some treacherous people, that he would be crucified, and that he'd wake up on the third day."

Yes, they remembered. Then they left the tomb and reported everything to the eleven, and others, too. These women included Mary of Magdala, Joanna, and Mary the mother of James. Other women as well narrated these things for the apostles. But their words made no sense to the apostles. They wouldn't believe them.[2]

So Peter left and ran to the tomb. He bent over and looked in and saw the linen wrappings.[3] Nothing more.[4] Then he went home amazed at what had happened.

Two of their number were going that day to a village called Emmaus, about seven miles from Jerusalem. They were discussing the events that had taken place, and while they were in conversation Jesus came along and walked with them. But they didn't recognize him.

He said, "What are you talking about on your walk?" They stopped and looked sad. One of them, Cleopas, said, "Are you the only person in Jerusalem who doesn't know what happened here recently?"

5 But Jesus makes clear again and again that his mission is to save humanity from its ignorant self-destruction. Humanity could still be saved, not through belief but by adopting Jesus's teachings and the love-based way of life that he calls "the kingdom."

6 Once again, angels announce a phase in the life and mission of Jesus: first, the annunciation to Mary, then the pronouncement to shepherds at the birth, and now the resurrection.

7 Retelling the history of who he was and how he came to be, Jesus instructs them on how to be in his presence now that he is resurrected. They are slow to understand, just as millions after them have been slow to grasp his message.

8 Apparently, the sacred story Jesus told was not enough to reveal himself to the men, but when he breaks bread, a symbol of human community, they recognize him. Here we get a hint of the importance of ritual and image.

"What happened?"

"Jesus of Nazareth. He was a prophet who said and did wonderful things in the presence of God and the people. The chief priests and leaders gave him a death sentence and crucified him. We were hoping that he would save Israel.[5] It has been three days since all this took place. A few of our women shocked us when they went to the tomb early in the morning and didn't find his body. They came and told us that they had a vision: Angels told them that Jesus is alive.[6]

"A few of those among us went to the tomb and found it just as the women had described it, but they didn't see Jesus."

Then Jesus said to the men, "You foolish men. You are slow to trust what the prophets have said. Wasn't it necessary for Christos to endure these things and to enter into his glory?"

Then, beginning with Moses and all the prophets, he explained everything about himself found in the scriptures.[7]

As they approached their destination, Jesus seemed to be going on. They urged him to stay. "Stay with us. It's almost twilight. The day is nearly over." He went in and stayed with them.

Sitting at the table, he took the bread and blessed it and broke it into pieces and gave the pieces to them. Suddenly their eyes opened up and they recognized him.[8] But then he vanished. Then they said to each other, "Were our hearts not aflame when he was speaking to us on the road and when he was explaining the scriptures?"

They got up and went back to Jerusalem right away and found the eleven and some others gathered together. These informed the two that the master had truly risen and had appeared to Simon. They, in turn, told about their experience on the road and how they recognized the master in the breaking of the bread.

Then, as they were speaking, he himself stood in their midst and said, "Peace be to you."

They were startled and frightened, like seeing a spirit.

9 We, too, can resurrect into a new way of life, having a renewed identity, while still being ourselves, still in the flesh, going on with our lives. Any of us can say, "Look! I'm an ordinary person. I have a body. I'm in this world. Yet I'm resurrected. I was dead in my soul, but now I'm alive."

10 This remarkable statement, "Do you have anything to eat?" spoken at this special moment, may have many implications: (1) Jesus wants to show that he is there in flesh and blood, (2) Jesus will be present soon in the breaking of bread, and (3) Jesus loves food. His Epicurean nature shows itself once more.

11 To some biblical experts fish is as important an image of the Jesus reality as bread. John Dominic Crossan writes: "There must have been originally a bread and fish Eucharist, a meal in which the risen Lord was present to the *general community* as a whole."

> —Crossan, *The Historical Jesus: The Life of a Mediterranean Jewish Peasant* (New York: HarperCollins, 1992), 401

12   *Rubber eraser*
     in the shape of
     the seated Buddha.

     He removes errors
     in my work,
     as he does so,

     he disappears.
> —John Mueller, "Rubber Eraser," in *What Book!? Buddha Poems from Beat to Hiphop,* edited by Gary Gach (Berkeley, CA: Parallax Press, 1998), 195

13 Jesus is gone, but the followers feel "great joy." He has blessed them, as they now form the body of his teaching, healing, and promise for humanity. He has now resurrected and ascended. Free from personal limitations, he is now present for the ages as a beacon for a utopian, conscious, cultural evolution of the human being.

He said, "Why are you upset? Why is there doubt in your hearts? Look at my hands and feet. See, it's really me. Touch me and see. A spirit doesn't have flesh and bones as I have, as you can see."[9]

After speaking, he showed them his hands and feet.

They were so surprised and happy that they could hardly believe it. He said, "Do you have anything here to eat?"[10]

They gave him some broiled fish, which he took and ate in front of them.[11]

Then he spoke again. "This is what I said while I was with you: Everything written about me in the law of Moses and the prophets and Psalms has to be fulfilled." Then he taught them how to understand the writings. He said, "It's written that Christos would be tortured to death and wake up on the third day, that *metanoia*, a profound change of heart, would be taught in his name to all people, starting in Jerusalem. You are witnesses to all of this. See, I'm giving you the promises of my Father, but you have to stay here in the city until you are filled with the power from above."

He guided them outside the city to Bethany. There he raised his hands and blessed them. And while he was blessing them he left them and was borne up into the sky.[12] After honoring him, they went back to Jerusalem with great joy[13] and spent their time in the temple praising God.

Acknowledgments

The *Book of Luke* was a joy to translate and reflect upon. I had indispensable help from Professor George Nickelsburg, whose generosity and expertise have no limit. As always, I'm fortunate to be working closely with my editors Emily Wichland and Jon O'Neal. I couldn't do the work without referring regularly to the writings of John Dominic Crossan, Robert Funk, Marcus Borg, George Aichele and Stephen D. Moore. The understanding and support of my wife Hari Kirin Khalsa and my children Ajeet Khalsa and Abe Bendheim sustain me in this long process of producing four books in the series. My hope is to entice readers familiar with the gospels to find new depth of meaning in them and readers who feel distant from these texts to discover their beauty and relevance.

Notes

Introduction to Gospel

1. Translations and writings on the Gospels often include chapter and verse when passages are cited. I do not include the verse because I want the reader to have a fresh, clear experience of the text. I hope that the absence of verse numbers will intensify the feeling of reading poetry, rather than prose While this may make it slightly more difficult to navigate the text, I think the emphasis on the poetic is more important.

2. John G. Neihardt, *Black Elk Speaks* (New York: Pocket Books, 1959), 25.

Introduction to the Book of Luke

1. John Dominic Crossan, *The Historical Jesus* (New York: HarperCollins, 1992), 341.

Suggestions for Further Reading

Aichele, George. *Jesus Framed*. London: Routledge, 1996.

Crossan, John Dominic. *The Essential Jesus*. San Francisco: HarperSanFrancisco,1989.

————. *The Historical Jesus: The Life of a Mediterranean Jewish Peasant*. New York: Harper-Collins, 1992.

————. *Jesus: A Revolutionary Biography*. San Francisco: HarperSanFrancisco, 1994.

Funk, Robert W. *Jesus as Precursor*. Missoula, MT: Society of Biblical Literature, 1975.

King, Karen L. *The Gospel of Mary of Magdala: Jesus and the First Woman Apostle*. Santa Rosa, CA: Polebridge Press, 2013.

Moore, Stephen D. *Mark and Luke in Poststructuralist Perspectives: Jesus Begins to Write*. New Haven, CT: Yale University Press, 1992.

Moore, Thomas. *Writing in the Sand: Jesus and the Soul of the Gospels*. Carlsbad, CA: Hay House, 2009.

————. *Gospel—The Book of Mark: A New Translation with Commentary—Jesus Spirituality for Everyone*. Nashville: SkyLight Paths, 2017.

————. *Gospel—The Book of Matthew: A New Translation with Commentary—Jesus Spirituality for Everyone*. Woodstock, VT: SkyLight Paths, 2016.

About the Author

Thomas Moore is the author of the best-selling book *Care of the Soul* and many other books on deepening spirituality and cultivating soul in every aspect of life. He has been a monk, a musician, a university professor, and a depth psychotherapist, and today he lectures widely on holistic medicine, spirituality, psychotherapy, and the arts. He lectures frequently in Ireland and has a special love of Irish culture.

He has a PhD in religion from Syracuse University and has won several awards for his work, including an honorary doctorate from Lesley University and the Humanitarian Award from Einstein Medical School of Yeshiva University. Three of his books have won the prestigious Books for a Better Life awards. He writes fiction and music and often works with his wife, Hari Kirin, who is an artist and yoga instructor. He writes regular columns for *Spirituality & Health* and the *Huffington Post*. For more about him, visit thomasmooresoul.com.

Thomas Moore is available to speak to your group or at your event. For more information, please contact us at publicity@skylightpaths.com or at (615) 255-2665.